Brain
COMPATIBLE
LEARNING
FOR THE BLOCK

Custom Edition for Army Junior ROTC

R. BRUCE WILLIAMS & STEVEN E. DUNN
FOREWORD BY ROBERT LYNN CANADY

Pearson
Custom
Publishing

SkyLight
Professional
Development

Cover designed and illustrated by David Stockman.

Taken from:

Brain-Compatible Learning for the Block
by R. Bruce Williams and Steven E. Dunn
Copyright © 2000 by SkyLight Training and Publishing Inc.
A Pearson Education Company
Arlington Heights, Illinois 60005

This special edition published in cooperation with Pearson Custom Publishing.

Printed in the United States of America

10 9 8 7 6 5 4

Please visit our web site at *www.pearsoncustom.com*

ISBN 0–536–67885-5

BA 995018

 PEARSON CUSTOM PUBLISHING
75 Arlington Street, Suite 300, Boston, MA 02116
A Pearson Education Company

To Jack, faithful and loyal life partner, whose never-ending
support helps me reach for the skies.—R.B.W.

To Allison, my wife and best friend, who processes all
of life with me and clarifies all my learning experiences.—S.E.D.

ACKNOWLEDGMENTS

I wish to show my appreciation to all the teachers who have worked with me these past few years as they have made the transition to block scheduling. Their stories of successes inspired me to write this book. Their stories of difficulties convinced me of the need for this book. Most of all I have been struck by the openness and courage these teachers embodied as they left the comfort of tried and true lesson plans in the tried and true bell schedule and journeyed forth into the uncharted territory of using new instructional strategies in block scheduling.

I thank my friend and co-author, Steve Dunn, for joining me on this wild ride of writing a book together. I have so appreciated the fresh instuctional tools and insights he has brought to this book.

So many have supported this venture. The enthusiasm and expertise of Peggy Kulling, our editor, has been unparalleled.

I also name Richard, Jim, John, and David as some of the many others who have encouraged me along.

—R.B.W.

*   *   *

I want to thank the thousands of students who taught me during the twenty years I was a classroom teacher. The variety of ways they learned made it clear to me that learning is a unique as each individual. I also want to thank the many inspiring educators with whom I worked as a consultant over the past ten years. Their demand for excellence motivated me to expand my learning and to try to be a better educator. I am continually awed by their love of learning, their dedication to their students, and their creativity in the teaching process. I especially want to thank the faculty at Logan High School, Logan, Utah, who gave me invaluable insights into the learning process and lesson design during the past year, especially Kathleen Cottle, Cathy Johnson, and Tim Cybulski. I am forever in the debt of the many outstanding teachers who devoted to my four children countless hours of their time. I also want to thank my co-author, Bruce Williams, for his friendship and for modeling how effective our lesson design can be. And finally, I want to thank my children, Meg, Bess, Joseph, and Daniel, who love me even though I spent more time at the computer during this writing process than with them. I'm proud to be their dad.

—S.E.D.

CONTENTS

FOREWORD

For the past ten-plus years it has been demonstrated in hundreds of schools across the nation that a school's climate and environment can be improved rather quickly just by altering a school's schedule. For example, in most schools we find that the number of referrals to the office is reduced when students each day spend fewer minutes under a time deadline in crowded spaces such as hallways, dressing rooms, and lunchrooms; obviously class tardies are reduced if each day students report to four blocks of classes rather than eight single periods of classes!

Although there have been modifications to some of the types of block schedules that Michael Rettig and I proposed in our 1995 book *Block Scheduling: A Catalyst for Change in High Schools,* the concept of block scheduling continues to be accepted by large numbers of administrators, teachers, parents, and students. There also is a growing collection of data from hundreds of individual schools that report increases in student performance based on factors such as improved grade point averages, attendance, and graduation rates, along with increases in the number of students taking advanced placement (AP) classes as well as increases in AP and ACT scores.

In spite of reported successes in over one hundred high schools, we still believe that the continued success of the block scheduling movement will be determined largely by the ability of teachers and administrators to work together to improve instruction. When extended time formats have been well utilized with appropriate instructional techniques, there has been genuine improvement in student achievement. This finding certainly can be documented in a relatively large number of individual schools throughout the country.

Needless to say, merely altering the time design by itself has not automatically resulted in improved student achievement. Most teachers have needed professional development opportunities and other resources to assist them in expanding their repertoire of teaching strategies so that they could make maximum use of these extended blocks of time. This book can be a resource to help teachers with this endeavor.

Regardless of the school's time schedule, what happens between individual teachers and students in classrooms is still most important. There is growing support that a well-designed school schedule can be a catalyst for critical changes—including instructional changes in classrooms—needed in high schools across America. We contend that staff development remains the key to the success of these instructional changes. Teachers must have multiple opportunities to develop active learning strategies in their various disciplines. Long periods of lecturing do not work; at a minimum, teachers must know how to make lecture more interactive. They need a repertoire of approaches to convey content in lively, challenging ways so that students develop both deep and long-term understandings of the concepts and skills that will make them successful not only in school but also after they leave today's classrooms.

In *Brain-Compatible Learning for the Block* R. Bruce Williams and Steven E. Dunn have summarized a decade of material on contemporary brain research and argue that block scheduling is compatible with what we know today of how to utilize students' multiple intelligences as well as what we know about how students learn best. The authors also show how curriculum, instruction, and assessment can be implemented effectively in an extended time format.

In each chapter, the authors provide sample lesson formats. These lesson plans, along with their suggested models for unit and lesson design, can assist teachers in navigating their way through the different world of teaching in extended time formats. This book is filled with numerous figures, charts, and graphics that clarify the text and make it a "Monday morning resource"; that is, a resource that teachers will want as a handy reference whether they are planning at home or during their planning time at schools. Ultimately, it is students who will benefit from teachers who make use of this resource text.

ROBERT LYNN CANADY
Professor Emeritus
University of Virginia and Senior Education Consultant
for State and National Programs for Education,
University of Virginia

PREFACE

This book results from a great deal of experience working with teachers at just about every stage of implementing instruction in the block. We believe it will be of great practical assistance in increasing student achievement in classrooms with extended time formats.

Brain compatible learning is a theory characterized by the natural progression everyone follows to learn. Ignoring each individual's best learning mode and demanding everyone learn in the same way, discourages rather than encourages learning. If students are left to their own design, they will learn when exposed to new and challenging ideas and skills that interest and excite them. A teacher's role is to facilitate the natural process each person follows to learn as well as inspiring students to challenge themselves to achieve greater understanding. That is why this book is is important. It provides JROTC instructors with the tools needed to bring brain compatible learning strategies into their classrooms.

Teachers using some form of extended time block tell us that good teachers will really shine in this situation. In a way, block scheduling is what the skilled teacher has been waiting for. Good teachers have always been those who are flexible, resourceful, and creative—all qualities and attributes that will serve them well in an extended block. On the other hand, under-skilled, lecture-dependant teachers are destined to experience great difficulty when confronted with double the class time. Often such teachers merely take two old lessons and paste them together to make one lesson. Or, teachers may present the usual forty-five to fifty minute lesson and have students do homework for the remainder of class time. Neither of these approaches makes effective use of the gift of more student contact time.

We believe that block scheduling is the best environment in which to fully utilize brain-compatible instructional techniques and approaches. Yet merely lengthening the time of each period will not make much difference. In fact, it may put obstacles in student achievement. The lengthened class time is only advantageous when additional and varied instructional strategies are employed so that curriculum content can move from disaggregated facts to meaningful information and relevant concepts. We have presented here several options and ideas, which have been informed by recent neuroscientific research, for creating lesson plans and units that make the most of extended time formats.

The incredible combination of military and real-life experiences JROTC instructors bring into their classrooms along with their skillful use of best learning strategies can make any JROTC classroom the most stimulating and exciting in the entire school. Students deserve the best learning environments we can provide them. And they deserve to be challenged by high expectations of performance and achievement. But high expectations without appropriate support and guidance can frustrate and intimidate rather than motivate student accomplishment. Teaching is a balancing act and effective JROTC instructors use all the instructional tools they have to achieve that balance. Wisdom comes from becoming aware of what and how we learned from our own experiences and then helping others along their journey. Great teachers are wise and continually search for and find the best ways to help each student learn.

We see this book as a real handbook, a practical toolbox for the teacher instructing in block scheduling or other alternative extended time format, and we hope that teachers and administrators will use it as such. We send you out on this journey of exploration to discover not only what increases your effectiveness as a teacher but what enhances the learning and achievement of your students.

This custom JROTC edition is designed to assist the JROTC instructor. New to this edition is a specific lesson example from the modified JROTC lesson plan format used in the revision of the JROTC curriculum. In addition, a blank template has been included to provide JROTC instructors with the opportunity to create their own brain compatible lessons. These additions make this edition a more powerful resource for the JROTC instructor.

—R. BRUCE WILLIAMS
—STEVEN E. DUNN

INTRODUCTION
Tools of the Trade

A lesson design is to a teacher what a recipe is to a chef, a blueprint to an architect, or a game plan to a coach. Not only does the recipe tell the chef what ingredients are needed, it also prescribes the amount of each ingredient, the sequence for combining the ingredients, and the preparation techniques required to prepare the dish. In similar fashion, an architect creates a construction blueprint on which are the types of materials needed to construct the building, the amount of each material, the construction plan, and the guidelines for construction. Coaches follow a similar process while preparing their teams. They choose the offense and defense that are most likely to counter the strengths of the opponents, they assign each athlete to the best playing position, and they rehearse the strategies to insure that their athletes have the competence and confidence to execute well.

Likewise, lesson plans guide teachers in selecting activities that work best for helping students understand lesson concepts and acquire new information, in determining how long to spend on each learning activity, and in deciding when each activity should be included during the learning process. Lesson plans are the recipes, blueprints, and game plans for engaging students in a successful learning process.

However, lesson plans are just that—plans. What really makes lessons come alive are the skillful strategies employed by teachers. The underpinnings for each successful lesson plan are the brain-compatible teaching or instructional strategies that work best to provide appropriate learning experiences for students. These strategies are the teacher tools. Not only do teachers need to select the tools for each lesson, they need to become more skillful

2

in the use of these tools. A comparative analogy is the architectural blueprint. Competent construction workers not only know how to read the blueprints, but they also know which tools to select for each part of the construction job, and they have the skills to use those tools correctly. Their ability to choose the appropriate tools from their "tool belt" for each part of their job and their expertise in the use of those tools will determine the quality of the finished construction project. The same principles apply to teachers. The lesson plan is lifeless until skilled teachers bring it to life by selecting their best tools from their teacher tool belts.

Brain-Compatible Learning for the Block is a highly practical resource for teachers, not just as a blueprint but as an instructional guide to creating one's own blueprints (lesson and unit plans). Each of the first five chapters provides a detailed sample Four-Phase lesson, which includes standards identified by James S. Kendall and Robert J. Marzano (1997) in their *Content Knowledge: A Compendium of Standards and Benchmarks for K–12 Education*.

The four phases of the lessons are *inquire, gather, process,* and *apply,* a design built upon the concepts of the "three-story intellect" and the processing model.

The purpose of the *inquire* phase is to help learners identify what they already know about the concept(s), information, or skill(s) to be covered in the lesson. Students explore what they know by determining past experiences that relate to the topic, by retrieving from long-term memory previously formed associations with the topic, and by identifying skills they have previously acquired. During this phase students discover what other students know about the lesson content. And just as important, students discern how they feel about the lesson topic, how motivated or reluctant they are, and what they would like to learn.

The primary purposes of the second phase of the lesson design, the *gather* phase, is to help students collect new information related to the lesson topic, to create a new schema or mental model, and to refine an existing schema. Strategies teachers employ during this phase need to engage students in learning experiences that add to or enlarge their knowledge base and that connect the new information to what they already know or understand. Teachers need to select tools that will guide students through the process of creating new schemas and refining previously formed schemas.

As a function of the *gather* phase, students experience activities that will assist the brain as it stores new information into long-term memory (Sprenger 1998). Teachers guide students beyond the process of rote memorization and help them create their own meaning. Comparing examples, targeting the similarities among examples, and helping students encode and organize the similarities among examples help students learn contextually.

To engage in thinking without acting upon what the brain is thinking about is antithetical to what the brain is designed to do—think and act (Sylwester 1995). During the *process* phase students are provided with an opportunity to knead and manipulate the knowledge and concepts, data, skill, technique, or behavior, ultimately molding them into a tool that they can use to carve out meaning from that which they encounter in real life. Strategies selected during this phase include complex activities that engage the whole student—cognitive, affective, and psychomotor—as part of the processing experiences (Bruer 1998). Such things as speaking, reading, writing, interacting, performing, planning, problem solving, and organizing need to be part of using all new information and skills.

The purpose of the *apply* phase is to use the tools forged in the previous phases in a relevant and practical context to create something new. The focus in this phase is to help students improve their proficiency under a variety of conditions or situations. The teacher engages in the direct teaching of transfer. Transfer can be presented as the ways the lesson content is connected to other disciplines, such as how a music lesson on fugues has applications to a math class or how the language arts lesson on Shakespeare's *Julius Caesar* is related to a speech or debate class. Transfer can also be related to the multiple intelligences, such as how an understanding of a math concept like trigonometry (logical/mathematical) can be used in solving problems related to putting a shot, platform diving, or uneven bars in gymnastics (bodily/kinesthetic). Generalization and transfer are recognizing problems in new and different settings. The apply phase connects the material to the real life of the student.

Brain-Compatible Learning for the Block is presented in six chapters. The first five chapters acquaint the reader with the tools (strategies and techniques) that will help them implement and ultimately design their own Four-Phase lesson and unit plans as set forth in the sixth chapter and in the samples provided throughout.

Chapter 1: Physiology and Philosophy provides an in-depth discussion of what recent research in the area of neuroscience seems to indicate about the brain's structure and multi-functionality and the implications for education.

Chapter 2: Block Scheduling: Time for Brain-Compatible Learning explores various alternative scheduling formats and the impact time has on learning.

Chapter 3: Content and Curriculum examines the weighty issue of content coverage and makes several practical suggestions for using the gift of time that alternative scheduling provides to delve deeply into content.

Chapter 4: Instruction: The Art and Science of Teaching in the Block focuses on brain-compatible educational principles and strategies that help teachers build a robust and exciting learning climate. In addition, ways in which an alternative schedule can make time for ongoing professional development are discussed.

Chapter 5: Assessment: Measuring Achievement and Growth in the Block balances the reality of standardized testing with the opportunity that authentic assessments provide to "catch" students learning.

Chapter 6: Four-Phase Lesson and Unit Design goes over the fine points of this innovative and dynamic design scheme. An outline of a sample unit is included.

Brain-Compatible Learning for the Block challenges and inspires teachers with concrete and practical ideas and the promise of an enriched learning environment for both students *and* teachers.

CHAPTER 1

PHYSIOLOGY AND PHILOSOPHY

Edelman's model of our brain as a rich, layered, messy, unplanned jungle ecosystem is especially intriguing…because it suggests that a junglelike brain might thrive best in a junglelike classroom that includes many sensory, cultural, and problem layers that are closely related to the real-world environment in which we live—the environment that best stimulates the neural networks that are genetically tuned to it.

—Robert Sylwester 1995, 23

The Brain's Structure and Functions

Because of the complexity of the brain's physiology, it is logical to assume its functioning is at least as complex. The brain has a myriad of interconnecting systems made for figuring out complexities. Current neuroscientific research appears to reveal that many of the traditional assumptions about how people learn, which were largely based on behavioralist theory, are faulty. As more is understood from research about how humans learn, it will become increasingly possible to discover better methods of facilitating learning (see chapter 4).

All attempts to summarize how the brain works fall short of both the complexity and the magnificence of how the brain is structured and how it functions. Any such effort will oversimplify the intricacies of the brain. However, it's important for teachers to be aware of the basic physiology of the brain in order to understand what neuroscience has to say.

There are three major regions of the brain: the brain stem (at the base), the limbic system (above that), and neocortex mushrooming out at the top. (see Figure 1.1 The Human Brain: Top to Bottom.)

The **brain stem** (sometimes called the reptilian brain) is considered to be the oldest part of the brain from an evolutionary standpoint. It follows then that much of the processing of basic survival instincts (respiration, digestion, and the "fight or flight" response) begins here.

The **limbic system**, once thought to be the exclusive repository of emotion, is now known to process not only emotional response but a number of highly cognitive functions including memory. Therefore, the connection between emotion and learning is great.

The **neocortex** (sometimes called the cerebral cortex or neurocortex) is believed by researchers to have grown out of the limbic system at some time in human evolution. Though not exclusively, the neurocortex is where higher-order and abstract thinking are processed and sensory input is comprehended (Goleman 1995). It attaches feeling and value to stimuli it receives. When students learn, it is the structure and chemistry of the nerve cells residing in the neurocortex that are changed (D'Archengelo 1998). Brain-compatible education is about making the connections that bring about actual changes in the brain's physiology. Ultimately, brain compatibility is acknowledging the way the brain processes stimuli and then designing activities, lessons, and units that complement and work with these processes.

The Human Brain: Top to Bottom

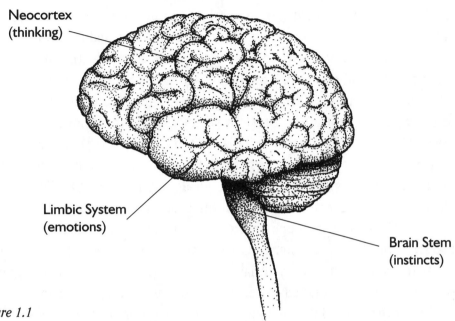

Neocortex
(thinking)

Limbic System
(emotions)

Brain Stem
(instincts)

Figure 1.1

Memory

The brain makes use of several kinds of memory systems. For the purpose of this discussion, two kinds of memory systems are highlighted: taxon and locale. Taxon memories are most clearly related to sheer rote memorization. Spelling words, multiplication tables, state and provincial capitals, and the bones of the hand are all examples of items that require sheer memorization and thus the function of the taxon memory system (Caine and Caine 1991).

Locale memories, on the other hand, are connected to events or happenings. Usually they are associated with emotions, relationships, and connections to other material. Locale memories can be thought of as configurations of information, or mental maps, which have the capacity to withdraw material deposited in the taxon memory. Getting information into taxon memory is an arduous task, however. Getting information into locale memory can be much less taxing on the brain (Sylwester 1995). In other words, the big picture of something is more related to the locale memory, which uses the intricate pieces, parts, or elements of the picture stored in taxon memory.

Consequently, the more connections and relationships established among pieces of information the more easily the information can be called forth and used. The fewer big-picture frameworks or connections or relationships there are, the more difficult it is for information to be accessed and employed. If connections and transferability are not enabled, then the student who memorizes grammatical rules, for example, has a difficult time using them to construct a cover letter (Caine and Caine 1991). There is a distinct disadvantage to relying solely on the short-term memory system; it cannot hold very much (Sylwester 1995). Furthermore, LeDoux (1996) suggests that while there is only one memory system supporting the taxon memory ability, there are multiple memory systems beyond the locale memory's ability. The brain clearly favors long-term memory and the locale memory ability.

The block offers an opportunity not only for the teacher to "cover the material" but for the teacher to create learning experiences that allow students to grapple with the material and make it their own. This very grappling with the material is related to getting the material into the locale memory system of the brain, into the long-term memory, where it has a much better chance of being rapidly accessed when needed.

Finding creative ways to structure the activities to engage the student in a significant learning experience becomes the real challenge for the teacher in a block format. Many teachers today just do not know any way to deliver material other than through a lecture. Because of this, devising ways—such as teacher planning teams who work on planning lessons together—to capitalize on the creativity present among teachers is absolutely imperative in facilitating the shift to a new time format.

Brain-Compatibility and Multifaceted Learning

The brain-compatible classroom depends upon, among other things, the teacher becoming a "brain-compatible" teacher. Teachers need to recognize each facet of an enriched learning experience (the Learner, the Content, and the Activity) to bring the concept of brain-compatibility into focus.

Nine Facets of Brain-Compatible Learning

   I. Learning becomes relevant through personal context.

   II. Learning is dependent upon motivation.

   III. Learning is reinforced through hands-on experience.

   IV. Learning requires linking new information to prior knowledge.

V. Learning is achieved more efficiently when information is "chunked."

VI. Learning is enhanced with time for reflection.

VII. Learning is retained longer when associated with senses and emotions.

VIII. Learning occurs for the greatest number in an environment that fosters and accommodates various ways of being smart.

IX. Learning is a high-energy activity.

Figure 1.2, "Brain-Compatibility in Focus," illustrates the interaction and relationship between brain-compatible learning, the learner, the content, and the activity.

The Learner

Most teachers are well-grounded in the content before setting foot in the classroom. Once there, however, the primary focus needs to be on the learn-

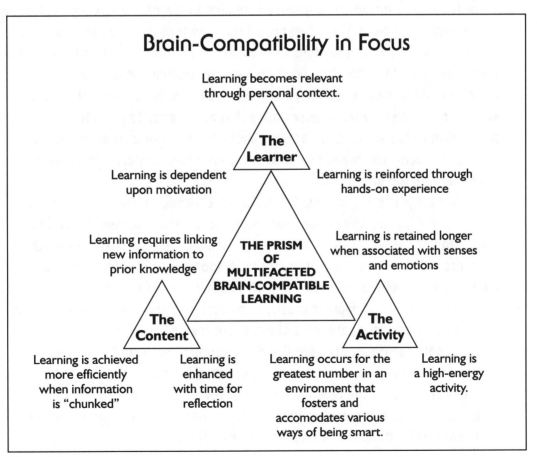

Brain-Compatibility in Focus

Learning becomes relevant through personal context.

The Learner

Learning is dependent upon motivation

Learning is reinforced through hands-on experience

Learning requires linking new information to prior knowledge

THE PRISM OF MULTIFACETED BRAIN-COMPATIBLE LEARNING

Learning is retained longer when associated with senses and emotions

The Content

The Activity

Learning is achieved more efficiently when information is "chunked"

Learning is enhanced with time for reflection

Learning occurs for the greatest number in an environment that fosters and accomodates various ways of being smart.

Learning is a high-energy activity.

Figure 1.2

ers they encounter. Who are they? What are their strengths and gifts? What are their weaknesses? What are their life experiences? What makes them tick? It is important to look not only at the characteristics and dynamics of the group but also those of each individual. Without some sense of who these learners are, it is impossible to create a brain-compatible classroom.

I. LEARNING BECOMES RELEVANT THROUGH PERSONAL CONTEXT

"Our brain is most efficient at recalling and using episodic memories that have important personal meanings" (Sylwester 1995, 96). Students are better able to understand information when they integrate learning with their own life experiences. The brain responds best in a learning environment when it can make the connection between the learning going on and real-life applications.

When learning is connected to material that is perceived to be useful in real life, the brain is more alert and pays more attention to that learning. It is more feasible to introduce a lesson or subject with a demonstration, video, or case study that "shows the relevance of the new topic to real-life concerns; and stimulates serious questions in each student's mind" in an extended time format (Fitzgerald 1996, 20). Teachers need to explicitly draw the connections to real-life even when they may seem obvious. New material is thus surrounded with an aura of importance that automatically provides its own motivation to the student. In fact, the more the student is engaged in the process of seeing the meaning and connection of the material presented to everyday life, the better it is.

Teachers preparing lessons for use in an expanded time block need to work hard at making the connections and the relevancy to real life crystal clear. Units or lessons can be introduced with a simple hook that helps the students see the connections to real life. A short video, a reference to a current news event, a reference to a TV character or to a music or movie star, a line from a piece of popular music, or a recent neighborhood or community event can all help students make the content material relevant.

Teachers can create thought-filled questions to help students make these connections. Engaging, complicated tasks can also energize student thinking so they can discover the relevancy on their own. With the help of their colleagues, teachers can come up with the kinds of "complex, interactive tasks" that require the student to grapple with the content.

Students come to school immersed in real life. Their own lives, television, and movies make it inescapable. Their brains are filled with real life before they walk into school. A student's real life context creates a tableau that educators recognize by showing how what they have to teach can assist the student in the journey through life.

II. LEARNING IS DEPENDENT UPON MOTIVATION

Students will file information in long-term memory when they are motivated by and interested in the new information. Attending to this new information does take energy and concentration; therefore, learning activities need to be designed to enhance motivation and pique student interest. "Memory is impossible without emotion of some kind, that emotion energizes memory. The practical consequence is that the enthusiastic involvement of students is essential to most learning" (Caine and Caine 1991, 57). Understanding what is motivational for students is critical to their successful learning.

Teachers can discern what motivates their particular students by doing the following:

- Simply asking individual students directly
- Paying attention to what the students like to write about
- Listening to the conversations going on in cooperative groupings
- Speaking informally with students before or after class
- Providing options, alternatives, and choices in assignments.

III. LEARNING IS REINFORCED THROUGH HANDS ON EXPERIENCE

Hands-on experience can incorporate many different skills, including practical, physical, and metacognitive, engaging students in discovery. Simulated or real experiences can elicit critical thinking as it applies to real-life situations. Hands-on experience can place the learning process into a context that is understood by students. Experience allows students to take concepts, skills, and information apart to understand how each part works and then put the parts together into a working whole. Long recognized as an integral part of the science curriculum, laboratories are crossing curricula. Technology/computer labs, science labs, language labs, art and music studios, school radio stations, TV-video production, and on-line and real-life writing labs are just some of the meaningful and authentic ways to demonstrate what students know in the fashion that best suits the way(s) they are smart.

The Content

Once teachers are acquainted with the students in their classrooms, they need to find ways to present the content in a manner that will connect with those students. Skillful and effective teachers

- Find out what students already know about the content
- Give the content material an illuminating framework
- Decide on a structure that speaks to their particular group of students.

IV. LEARNING REQUIRES LINKING NEW INFORMATION TO PRIOR KNOWLEDGE

Exploring and asking questions about previously learned and understood material helps students build a bridge from their current knowledge to new information. The key is to help students make connections between the new material and the knowledge they already possess. The brain has a limited capacity to take in unrelated, disconnected facts. On the other hand, the brain has an almost limitless capacity to incorporate material it can connect and relate to knowledge already learned. To ignore this natural memory capacity is to abandon what the student can bring to the learning.

The brain's natural memory capacity is enhanced when the individual becomes engaged in the process of organizing or creating the connections. Very often teachers deliver material without connecting it to that which has been previously learned or without engaging the student in making the connections. Stating beforehand to the student what the connections are without engaging the student in making the connections is not helpful. More time coupled with appropriately crafted lessons offers more opportunities for students to relate new information to old information.

V. LEARNING IS ACHIEVED MORE EFFICIENTLY WHEN NEW INFORMATION IS "CHUNKED"

The brain automatically connects information that appears related. The brain searches for patterns in the new information it receives, and if something appears familiar, it is connected to what is already stored. By *chunking* information together, the brain begins to form a concept, a schema, an idea, or an understanding of the experience or information. The brain's ability to form patterns is unlimited and includes such things as how a nonfiction book is different from fiction, what makes an animal a dog and not a cat, what a right angle triangle is, what the characteristics of a good teacher are, what defines happiness, what the purpose of science is, and so on.

The brain has a natural drive to discern meaning in information and events as well as to discern patterns and create order out of what seems like chaos. When the brain is given permission to seek out patterns and meaning, a great deal of learning occurs.

A key point is how much the brain resists the forcing of patterns that don't make sense. The brain's inclination is to find the patterns and create the meaning that makes sense for itself—not what makes sense to someone else. Another key point is that these are qualities of every brain. How a brain creates patterns, what patterns it creates, how a brain figures out meaning, what meanings it creates—all of this will vary greatly from brain to brain. What is consistent is that every brain is wired to create patterns and to figure out meaning (Caine and Caine 1991).

VI. LEARNING IS ENHANCED WITH TIME FOR REFLECTION.

Reflection and metacognition can greatly aid in the whole effort of finding the patterns and drawing out the meaning of information and events (Caine and Caine 1997). Metacognitive activities, which on the surface may appear to take time away from learning valuable content, are actually activities that can enhance content learning and cause the material that has been reflected upon to become part of the learner's long-term memory system. Group discussions, metacognitive questioning, logs and journals, and graphic organizers are helpful processing tools and can perhaps be most efficiently employed during extended time blocks. For some students, it is only when time is allowed for reflection that lasting connections to the material are made.

The Activity

Taking into account the learner and the content, the teacher needs to think about the particular strategies and tactics that will best carry out the instruction of the content. Teachers might ask themselves the following questions: How does this content link to the senses and the emotions? (*All content* can in some way be linked to the senses and emotions.) How can a teacher utilize the various intelligences to capitalize on the many ways *these* students are smart? What kind of energy and intensity will assist this learning?

VII. LEARNING IS RETAINED LONGER WHEN ASSOCIATED WITH THE SENSES AND EMOTION

New information, when associated with sight, sound, smell, and emotion, is retained for a longer period of time.

Ways to Make Senses a Part of the Learning Experience

Students can

- Share what their perceptions or impressions of India, Pakistan, or other countries on the subcontinent are at the beginning of a lesson or unit while the teacher burns incense
- Gather information about the parts of a flower using artist Georgia O'Keeffe's paintings of flowers
- Gain a sensory and emotional connection to the 1920s, or any other time, by listening to music, wearing clothing, or playing with toys or sporting goods from that period
- Taste or make simple foods eaten in Latin America as a part of a lesson or unit on that region

Sensory experiences provide more stimulus input that increases the chance that material will move into long-term memory.

Emotions play a crucial role in the process of learning and getting information into memory systems. Emotions are central to eliciting attention, and attention is crucial to effective learning and memory (Sylwester 1995). Unfortunately, schools have had great difficulty understanding the role of emotion. In fact, educators have often banished emotion from the classroom, leaving the classroom a passionless and sterile place. Within the confines of the core curriculum, emotion and the show of emotion have been seen as a transgression. Emotion was left to be explored in non-core subject areas such as "the arts, PE, recess, and the extracurricular program[s]" (Sylwester 1995, 72). In so doing, the very necessary component of emotion is left out of the learning process. "When we ignore the emotional components of any subject we teach, we actually deprive students of meaningfulness" (Caine and Caine 1991, 58). In other words, emotions play a vital role in the entire process of creating meaning. On a more elemental level, "[e]motions are also crucial to memory because they facilitate the storage and recall of information" (Rosenfield 1988, 92).

All of the above suggest that recognizing and embracing the power of constructive emotion is the key to enhancing student motivation and learning in the classroom. One reason why it is so crucial for educators to pay attention to the role of emotions is the power they can hold over cognitive abilities. According to brain researchers, this is because of the nature of the connections between the emotional systems and the cognitive systems.

Paying attention only to cognitive activities in the classroom neglects a crucial factor now becoming clear to contemporary brain research: "[E]motion and cognition are best thought of as separate but interacting mental functions mediated by separate but interacting brain systems" (LeDoux 1996, 69). So the call is clear: Paying attention to the role of emotions is a way not only to care for the students but to facilitate their learning as well.

Questions that Invite Constructive Emotions Into the Classroom

The following questions can be posed by the teacher to elicit classroom discussion or used as "rhetorical" questions students can respond to in their reflection journals.

- Which part of the lesson today did you like? In which part of the lesson did you struggle most?
- If you were to select a piece of music to play as background for this story, lesson, or experiment, what would it be? Why would you choose that?
- How do you suppose the Reverend Martin Luther King, Jr. felt while incarcerated in the Birmingham jail? What would have been your feelings if you had been there with him? What would your feelings have been if you were Dr. King?
- What emotions did Pablo Picasso likely experience when he created the masterpiece *Guernica*?
- What emotional shifts did you notice in this character? What enabled or caused the emotional shifts? What causes shifts in your emotions (positive to negative as well as negative to positive)?

VIII. LEARNING OCCURS IN AN ENVIRONMENT THAT ACCOMMODATES AND FOSTERS VARIOUS WAYS OF BEING SMART

Howard Gardner (1983), very early in his psychological research, became concerned with the narrow definitions of intelligence being used by educators and researchers. The more he researched persons possessed of full brain capabilities as well as with those impaired by brain injury, the more he began to see different intelligence capabilities emerging in different persons. Eventually Gardner (1995) identified eight intelligences, which include visual/spatial, logical/mathematical, verbal/linguistic, musical/rhythmic, bodily/kinesthetic, interpersonal/social, intrapersonal/introspective, and naturalist. Chapter 4 describes multiple intelligence theory in depth as it relates to teaching in the block. See also Figure 4.5, "Gardner's Eight Intelligences."

There is both good news and a profound challenge for educators in Gardner's theory. "The good news is that each of us has all of these intelligences" and "[w]e have the ability to enhance and amplify our intelligence" (Lazear 1991, *ix*). The challenge lies in the need for educators to perceive and encourage the rich intelligence gifts of every student in their classrooms and to discover ways to strengthen the less developed intelligences in these same students.

Expanded blocks of time can give the teacher additional opportunities to create learning activities that take advantage of more than just the logical/mathematical and verbal/linguistic intelligences in any given class period. In fact, creating activities that connect with several of the intelligences in one block period can be precisely what will keep all students interested and attentive. Consequently, the content can come alive in ways not possible when a student is just listening (using verbal/linguistic intelligence) to thirty to forty minutes of a teacher lecture. Such a use of a variety of learning is another way to help the students make the content in the classroom their own.

IX. LEARNING IS A HIGH-ENERGY ACTIVITY

"The brain is about two percent of an adult's body weight, but demands about twenty percent of the body's energy" (D'Arcangelo 1998, 21). Short-term memory, the process in the brain where associating, connecting, categorizing, and meaning-making of new concepts occurs, requires concentrated focus and attention. New information begins to decay after thirty seconds if no rehearsal is applied. Therefore, it is important that new information is revisited several times in a variety of different ways. The high intensity of receiving new information needs to be followed with a time of lower intensity reflection. Pulsed learning follows the natural pattern of high-energy attention and low-energy processing or mental meanderings.

While learning requires a great deal of energy from students, that energy must be sparked and sustained by the energy present in the classroom. Teachers who welcome the student, lessons that incorporate a variety of activities that are in tune with content objectives, and teachers who model enthusiasm can increase the energy present in the classroom, which in turn helps fuel student concentration and attention.

Block Scheduling and the Brain-Compatible Learning Climate

One of the critical aspects of learning that comes from brain research is that throughout history human learning has taken place in a complex environment (Bruer 1998). A complex environment is one that is filled with limitless wonders, surprises, experiences, and observations whether that environment is government buildings in Washington, D.C., or a small private farm in South Dakota. The brain is adapted for making meaning out of the complexities of its environment. When the classroom is a complex, dynamic environment, students can engage in activities that demand several brain and thought processes simultaneously. When this occurs, energy rises, motivation intensifies, and learning increases. Such things as engaging in debates, working with a small group of students to synthesize notes onto a graphic organizer, taking field trips to museums, small businesses or factories performing laboratory and field experiments, and constructing models are all examples of complex environments.

Seeing the linkages between the emotional and cognitive centers of the brain makes it clear that the atmosphere for learning is more crucial than may have previously been understood. An emotionally supportive environment can actually enhance the higher thinking processes of the brain. Block scheduling can enable more activities and learning experiences that engage higher-order thinking and problem solving. A school needs to consider the block if it believes that an alternative extended schedule could involve more and more students in significant learning activities.

Greater variety and flexibility occur in the classroom as more choices are offered to the student. In order to harness students' interests and skills, schools need to begin to match the variety, flexibility, complexity, and vitality of life outside the classroom (Caine and Caine 1991).

Expanded blocks of time can permit the teacher, often focused only on the content nature of the curriculum, to add multiple intelligence arenas, thinking skills, and social skills to the focus in the classroom. Once again, this has the potential of reshaping the classroom into a dynamic, interactive center of learning. Teachers working in the block report that in their experience a greater percentage of students want to come to school when this kind of dynamic, lively center of learning is taking place in classrooms. An additional comment is that such a classroom engages students who were never able to be engaged in thirty to forty minutes of lecture—thus creating classrooms compatible with the rich diversity of student populations.

Sample Four-Phase Lesson #1 acknowledges the way the brain processes information and makes the most of time in the block by utilizing brain-compatible learning techniques as they relate to multifaceted learning. Note the four phases mentioned in the introduction: *inquire, gather, process, apply*. The activities in the inquire phase of the lesson plan each raise consciousness of the brain as well as explore what students already know about the brain. Both of the activities in the gather phase encourage the students to amass and pull together relevant information. In the process phase, students discern the meaning from the information by using a graphic organizer. Finally, in the apply phase, they go one step further in higher-order thinking by creating a rubric for a student presentation of the material.

What's On Your Mind? is a biology lesson, with curriculum connections to psychology, technology, and physical education. The biology teacher may invite a psychology or physical education teacher or a local therapist, sport psychologist, or social worker to participate in the class. The integrated curricular focus for this lesson is psychology and physical education; however, the focus could be chemistry and drugs or health issues like Alzheimer's. The "reflect" component of the process phase can be used as a spring board to a service-learning project. The authentic assessment tool built into the *process* phase is a rubric for evaluating student presentations.

Sample Four-Phase Lesson Plan

What's On Your Mind?

Level: Secondary

Curriculum Integration: Biology (Anatomy and Physiology), Psychology, Technology, and Physical Education

Multiple Intelligences

- ❑ Bodily/Kinesthetic
- ☑ Interpersonal
- ☑ Intrapersonal
- ☑ Logical/Mathematical
- ❑ Musical
- ❑ Naturalist
- ☑ Verbal/Linguistic
- ☑ Visual/Spatial

Content Standards

LIFE SCIENCE

Knows the general structure and functions of cells in organisms

BEHAVIORAL SCIENCE

Understands that interactions among learning, inheritance, and physical development affect human behavior

LIFE SKILLS

Understands and applies basic principles of logic and reasoning
Performs self-appraisal

TECHNOLOGY

Uses methods of information-gathering on the Internet
Identifies capabilities and limitations of technology
Uses safe and ethical behavior on the Internet

PHYSICAL EDUCATION

Uses movement concepts and principles in the development of motor skill

INQUIRE PHASE
20 MINUTES

Inquire Activity 1

Objective: Students participate in "Student Tic-Tac-Toe" energizer.

ATTEND

The teacher asks . . .

- What happens to your thoughts when you're excited, nervous, or scared?
- What happens to your actions or your skills under the same situations?

The teacher suggests. . .

- As you play this energizer, observe what happens to the other students. What emotions do you recognize? What behaviors do you see? What do you hear students saying?
- What feelings do you experience?
- What behaviors do you exhibit?

EXPERIENCE: "STUDENT TIC-TAC-TOE"

Figure 1.3 "Student Tic-Tac-Toe" describes the rules and game format.

REFLECT

The teacher asks . . .

- How did students respond when they were unable to form a line and lost a round?
- How did they respond when they won?
- What happened to your thoughts and your feelings as you competed for a square and tried to form a line? How did you behave? Why?
- What kind of relationship exists in the human brain among thoughts, feelings, and behaviors?

Student Tic-Tac-Toe

The teacher or student leader prepares for the game by...

- Creating large tic-tac-toe grids on the floor using masking tape—one grid for every two groups created. Each quadrant should be large enough to comfortably accommodate a standing person with both arms outstretched.
- Asking for two or three volunteers to serve as game referees. (The number of referees should be based on the number of students playing the game. Additional referees can be used and rotated in to make sure the teams have an equal number of players.)
- Forming teams (of six to ten persons) of equal size
- Instructing students to count off within their teams
- Directing teams to choose a grid and stand across from another team on that same grid.

Informing teams of the rules of the game as follows:

- The teacher or student leader randomly calls out three numbers one through six (or one through the largest number present on the team). The numbers should be written down.
- The three players from each team run into the grid and try to form a vertical, horizontal, or diagonal line. Players may not attempt to create a line directly parallel to the side where they were standing.
- Teammates outside the grid may yell out encouragement to their teammates but not disparaging remarks to their opponents.
- Referees settle all disputes over who was there first.
- When a tic-tac-toe line is formed a point is awarded to that team.
- All persons leave the grid.
- The process is repeated by calling out different number combinations.
- The referees assigned to each grid keep score for both teams.

Figure 1.3

Inquire Activity Option A (When two options are offered, choose one.)

Objective: Students draw from memory several brain structures.

ATTEND

The teacher asks . . .

- What are the parts of the brain that you can recall?
- Is the brain's structure and function more like a computer, a jungle, or a tossed salad? Why?

EXPERIENCE: "PICTURE THIS"

Students . . .
- In small groups of three to four, work together to draw the brain and several brain and central nervous system structures they have previously studied including Brodmann's areas, precentral and postcentral gyrus, brain stem, motor units, and any other parts they recall.
- Combine their small group with another small group to share their visuals.
- Repeat the sharing process one or two times.

The teacher . . .
- Asks a group to present their visual to the class and leads a short discussion on the various areas.
- Clarifies any misconceptions and reinforces the connection between thoughts, physical movements, and behavior.

Inquire Activity Option B

Objective: Class prepares a KWL chart on the multifunctional brain.

ATTEND

The teacher poses the following questions, reinforces correct responses, and mediates misconceptions...
- What is a KWL chart?
- How is it used?
- When have you used it before?

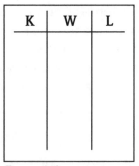

K	W	L

Figure 1.4

EXPERIENCE: "GROUP KWL"

The teacher . . .
- Leads the students in creating a class KWL chart on the multifunctional brain.

Students . . .
- offer responses to the KNOW column and WANT to know column, leaving the what you LEARNED column to be completed later.

REFLECT

The teacher asks the following questions . . .

- What new insights have you gained already about the multifunctional role of the brain?
- How do you know when you have learned something? In other words, how do you know you know?
- How might understanding various brain structures and functions help you understand yourself and others?

GATHER PHASE
25 MINUTES

Gather Activity

Objective: Students engage in an information gathering of specific brain terms and mental health concepts on the Internet.

The teacher . . .

- Divides the class into two groups, A and B (or students select a group). Group A's, small groups of three or four students, are assigned a neuroanatomy Web site and Group B's, small groups of three or four students, are assigned a mental health or psychology concepts Web site. Both A and B groups gather information at the same time.
- Locates and bookmarks appropriate neuroanatomy and mental health Web sites in advance of beginning the lesson (see Appendix). The number of sites the teacher provides should exceed the number of small groups. PLEASE NOTE: Teachers need to explore and monitor any Web sites they want their students to visit in advance of assigning the task.

ATTEND

The teacher focuses student attention by giving the following direction:

- Think of ways you could visually represent the information you find on the Web sites.

EXPERIENCE: "INTERNET INVESTIGATION PART 1: ALL "A" GROUPS"

Students . . .

- Are assigned a neuroanatomy Web site to explore in groups of three or four. Each group may explore only one site (jigsaw), or each group may explore each site.
- Study new information on the brain and prepare a demonstration of their understanding.
  - Take notes on, download, or print out information of importance/relevance.
  - Organize the information in a way that makes sense to them by using a graphic organizer (see chapter 4).

ATTEND

The teacher asks students the following questions . . .

- What's the difference between the brain and the mind?
- What does mental health mean?
- Create a group definition of depression, anxiety, and disorder.

EXPERIENCE: "INTERNET INVESTIGATION PART 2: ALL 'B' GROUPS"

Students are assigned a mental health–related Web site to explore in groups of three or four. Each group may explore only one site (jigsaw) or each group may explore each site. If a jigsaw activity is chosen, an additional "Gather experience" would have to occur so that the groups could share information.

REFLECT

Teachers ask the following questions . . .

- What are the functions of some specific brain structures you can identify?
- How do you perceive the brain differently as you learn more about its many functions?
- How did the various Web sites help you understand the various brain structures and functions?
- Which sites were most helpful to you? Why?

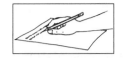

PROCESS PHASE
30 MINUTES

Process Activity 1

Objective: Students prepare a graphic organizer on the multifunctional brain and mental health (see chapter 4, Figure 4.7).

ATTEND

The teacher asks the following question to focus on the next experience . . .

- What immediate connection can you make between the structure of the *brain* and the mental health of the *mind*? Are these direct or indirect connections?

EXPERIENCE: "THE BRAIN/MIND EQUATION"

Students . . .

- Prepare a graphic organizer (sequence or flow chart, matrix, fishbone, concept map, mind map, or any other appropriate form) by working in groups of four (two students from group A and two from group B) that shows the interplay between the multifunctional brain and mental health.

REFLECT

The teacher asks the following questions:

- How did preparing the graphic organizer with your group help you understand the information more clearly?
- What did you learn about the brain and cognitive therapy that you think most people don't know?
- What will you be more aware of regarding your brain and your thoughts, feelings, and behaviors?

Process Activity 2

Objective: Students, along with the teacher, decide on the criteria for a well-presented distillation of the information students worked with in this lesson.

ATTEND

The teacher asks . . .

- What would an excellent presentation that sums up the lesson's content look like?

EXPERIENCE: "PERFORMANCE CRITERIA"

As a class, students . . .

- Decide upon a presentation rubric that the "audience" and the teacher will fill in during the *apply* phase to evaluate students' group presentations (see chapter 5). Figure 1.5 "Group Presentation Rubric" provides an example of such a rubric.

REFLECT

The teacher asks the following questions for students to contemplate and answer in their metacognitive journals . . .

- What will you have to do to help your group have a successful presentation?
- What have you learned from previous presentations that will help you with this one?
- How do you think your group will perform?

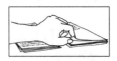

APPLY PHASE

15 MINUTES

Objective: Students present the information they recalled and uncovered in the lesson in a creative and interesting way.

Apply Activity

ATTEND

The teacher . . .

- Calls on one to three small groups of four to present their graphic organizers to the class. (The remaining groups will do their presentations during the next class session.)

    or

- Separates the small groups into two or three divisions (two to three small groups in a division and each small group presents to the other one or two groups in their division.

Group Presentation Rubric			
	Not Quite (1)	Okay (3)	Way Cool! (5)
All group members participated			
Information presented is accurate			
Information is deliberately organized			
Presentation is logical and sequential			
Visuals are clear and easily seen			
Presentation is creative and informative			
Presentation connects previously presented information			
One main concept is explored			
Includes audience participation			

Comments: Total Score

                                                              A = 27–30
                                                              B = 24–26
                                                              C = 21–23

Figure 1.5

EXPERIENCE: "PRESENTING..."

Students present their graphic organizers.

REFLECT

The teacher chooses from the following questions that may be answered as part of a class discussion if time allows or in the students' reflection journals . . .

- What excites you most about what you learned today?
- What do you want to do differently in your life as a result of your new understandings?
- How can you help someone who is having trouble handling their negative thoughts, emotions, and behaviors?
- What group could benefit from seeing your presentation? Why?
- Complete the "L" column (what you LEARNED) on the KWL begun in the *inquire* phase at the beginning of the day's lesson.

Students complete the following activity at home . . .

- Identify the brain anatomy and physiological mechanisms involved in these four scenarios:
  (1) Actors' stage "fright"   (2) Athletes "choking"
  (3) Students' test "panic"   (4) Crime victim "freezing"
- Include what happens to people cognitively, emotionally, physiologically, and behaviorally when they suffer the above conditions.

CHAPTER 2

BLOCK SCHEDULING
TIME FOR BRAIN-COMPATIBLE LEARNING

The classroom environment that best facilitates the full development of the intelligences is sometimes called "brain compatible." For the brain to function fully, it is beneficial for the classroom to provide five elements: trust and belonging, meaningful content, enriched environment, intelligence choices, and adequate time.

—Carolyn Chapman 1993, 9

Adequate Time

The first four elements of brain-compatible learning to which Carolyn Chapman (1993) alludes (trust and belonging, meaningful content, enriched environment, and choices) are dependant upon the fifth, adequate time (see Figure 2.1). Increasingly, educational professionals are exploring the concept of block scheduling to meet the need for time.

To clarify what is meant by block scheduling, it is informative to be reminded of the traditional bell schedule. Elementary schools generally work on their own system of large time blocks, leaving the individual teachers the flexibility to pace and plan curriculum according to the needs of the class and the material. In middle and secondary schools, however, students change classes every forty-three to fifty minutes seven to ten times a day. (Shorter class times naturally mean more class changes.) A student attends classes in six or seven subjects a day, shifting classes and passing through the halls that many times. In contrast, block scheduling often provides ninety to one hundred minutes for each class period. Thus, there are only four class periods a day: two in the morning and two in the afternoon. (See Figure 2.4 "4 by 4 Schedule.") A student has only four subjects a day instead of six or seven. In general, teachers on the block then teach only three subjects a day instead of five or six.

Research indicates that traditional shorter classes cause teachers to spend more than thirty percent of each class reviewing facts presented in the previous class. This is due primarily to the fact that students are not allowed the processing time needed to embed information into long-term memory (Semb and others 1993). Further, in conventional fifty minute classes only about twenty-eight minutes, or a little more than fifty percent of class time, is devoted to academic or instructional activities. The balance of the time is given over to "transitional activities" such as settling in, taking attendance, and collecting homework (Seifer and Beck 1984). Multiply the time spent in such activities by the number of different courses per day, and it is easy to see why adequate time is an elusive concept in the context of the traditional schedule.

The Benefits of Time

To paraphrase Joseph Carroll (1994), block scheduling is not about time; it is about the relationship between time and learning. While more time favors

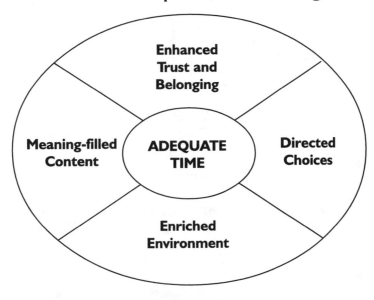

Five Elements of Brain-Compatible Learning

Figure 2.1

Adapted from *If the Shoe Fits…How to Develop Multiple Intelligences in the Classroom* by Carolyn Chapman. © 1991 by IRI/Skylight Training and Publishing, Inc. Reprinted with permission of SkyLight Professional Development, Arlington Heights, IL.

brain-compatible learning, it does not necessarily in and of itself bring about greater student cognition and performance. More time *is,* instead, an opportunity to employ the best brain-compatible practices to instruction, thereby achieving the greatest possible results.

There is only one reason to implement block scheduling: Because it meets the needs of the students. On the other hand, the resulting meaningful benefits of larger blocks of time for students include enhanced trust and belonging, directed choices, an enriched learning environment, and meaning-filled content. Following are just a few ways more time and brain-compatible learning strategies can work in concert to bring about the desired result—fully realized, thinking students. (See Figure 2.2 "Expanding on the Five Elements of Brain-Compatible Learning.")

Enhanced Trust and Belonging

As discussed in the previous chapter, emotion plays an essential role in the learning process. The need for an environment that recognizes and supports

Expanding on the Five Elements of Brain-Compatible Learning

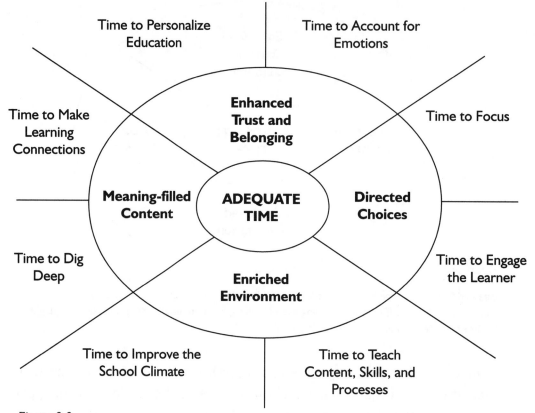

Time to Personalize Education

Time to Account for Emotions

Time to Make Learning Connections

Enhanced Trust and Belonging

Time to Focus

Meaning-filled Content

ADEQUATE TIME

Directed Choices

Time to Dig Deep

Enriched Environment

Time to Engage the Learner

Time to Improve the School Climate

Time to Teach Content, Skills, and Processes

Figure 2.2

student comfort, confidence, and camaraderie is increasingly important. Brain-compatible teaching strategies are informed by such knowledge, and block scheduling allows time for those strategies to be optimally exercised.

TIME TO PERSONALIZE EDUCATION

In the past, students received a great deal of emotional support from their local communities, their churches, their neighbors, and their extended families. As times have changed, such social and economic structures have themselves changed. Schools feel the ripple effect of this change in the attitudes and baggage students carry with them into the schoolroom. Now, because there is often little emotional support in middle school and secondary school students' lives, school needs to be a place where that kind of support can materialize—both for the students and the adult members of the school community alike. Unfortunately, the very time during which students undergo the greatest personal change, adolescence, is the same time they are abruptly moved from the elementary school environment where they have fewer class changes per day and a greater personal connection to their teachers to an environment where they must deal with seven to nine different teachers per day and conceivably 180 different classmates. A personal connection between an adult at school and his or her students may be the single most crucial factor in preventing students from dropping out of school (Shore 1995). An increased level of positive student-teacher relationship actually helps "underachieving" and "at-risk" students (Brett 1996).

The Human Factor

A block format enables the teacher to turn attention to the student as a human being. The block format can enable a human connection to occur when the teacher uses brain-compatible practices such as cooperative learning and service learning that help develop the intrapersonal and interpersonal intelligences. Personal connections encourage lifelong learning and enhance self-esteem, both of which are more important today then ever before. Genuine positive personal connections strengthen the school and the larger community, which is the ultimate goal of education.

TIME TO ACCOUNT FOR EMOTIONS

Research has shown the necessity of including emotions in the brain-compatible classroom. Lessons and classrooms that incorporate emotions can actually stimulate learning. One simple way to do this is for teachers to ask questions that directly relate to emotion:

- How do you feel about what this character did in this story?
- How do you feel about what this historical figure did?
- What emotions have you experienced while watching this video excerpt?
- What emotions do the characters display in this chapter?
- When have you felt something like what this character felt?

The key is for the teacher to pay close attention to students' answers, making sure that they are indicative of true emotions. "I felt confused" is more of an answer about unclear thinking than about emotions. "I was upset and angry." "I was frustrated." "I was delighted." "I was excited." These are all answers that indicate the expression of true emotion. Another simple way to tap into emotions is by learning what issues, ideas, topics, projects, hobbies, and whatever else ignites student enthusiasm. Tying learning to student interests can provide the emotional component that fuels student motivation to learn. Service learning, project learning, and case studies are profitable learning encounters because they each begin by beckoning emotions into the inquiry or exploration and then channeling those emotions into a well-defined learning task and experience. (Chapter 3 explains service learning, project learning, and case studies in depth.)

On the other hand, schools that use fear and coercion will not bring about the best results in learning and achievement. The threat of poor grades or temporary expulsion does not enhance student learning. In fact, William Glasser's (1990) research asserts that coercion can at best enable students to accomplish elemental, uncomplicated tasks and may actually impede the higher-order thinking that characterizes true understanding. Support and high challenge enable the kind of problem-solving skills and original thinking that today's modern technology-driven society demands from its students as well as its adults.

Teachers using expanded time block are able to create activities that can truly motivate and engage the learner because they involve the whole person. Students who

- do not handle sitting quietly for lectures have the opportunity to move around during activities and projects.
- love to talk to fellow students from time to time can do this during structured group work.
- want to share their feelings can do so during the conversations teachers lead.

Brain-compatible learning is more than just learning facts and information. Facts and information by themselves can be dry and boring. However, when facts and information become connected to practical situations, when they are rooted in real life, which naturally includes emotions, then the facts and information come alive and invite the student into more and more learning.

Directed Choices

It is becoming increasingly apparent from recent research that student learn at different paces and experience learning on their own terms. The teacher in an extended class period has the time and has hopefully amassed the professional resources to present students with challenging and stimulating learning experiences (options) that engage them fully in their own learning.

TIME TO FOCUS

Many teachers experience the seven- or eight-period day as rushed and hurried. Likewise, students are barely getting into material when the bell rings and it is time to go to the next class for a repeat of settling in, a dose of content, an assignment for the next day, and then another bell. "Assuming a seven-period day, a homeroom, and lunch, a typical student will be in nine locations pursuing nine different activities in a six and a half-hour school day. If the schedule includes physical education, he or she may have changed clothes twice and showered once....It produces a hectic, impersonal, inefficient instructional environment" (Carroll 1994, 5). Traditional schools have become some of the worst environments possible for enabling concentration and focus, which is true for both the student and the teacher.

What Robin Fogarty (1996, 1) suggests is echoed by countless teachers already teaching in some form of block scheduling. "These larger allotments of time allow students to concentrate their energies intensely on a single focus—the subject matter addressed during the block of time. In other words, the schedule itself encourages more involved, more active, and more student-initiated learning" (1996,1). Greater concentration occurs just by virtue of the fact that there are fewer hall changes. Hall changes can be unsettling and permit disorder, making it difficult for students to move into class and begin focusing immediately. In addition, the extended time block permits the kinds of activities and projects that engage students and draw forth the concentration and focus needed to accomplish learning.

Sharpening Focus

Focus does not happen automatically. It does not happen automatically in a forty-five minute class period, and it does not happen automatically in a ninety-minute class period either. Michaly Csikszentmihalyi (1990) has coined the term "flow" to describe a state where one's mental focus and one's emotional focus are linked together and engaged in learning. "Because flow emerges in the zone in which an activity challenges people to the fullest of their capacities, as their skills increase it takes a heightened challenge to get into flow. If a task is too simple, it is boring; if too challenging, the result is anxiety rather than flow" (Goleman 1995, 93). Such a state of student attention allows for the optimal and most sustainable learning experiences.

In an extended time schedule, each day the context is set reminding the student of the direction and intention of the unit, what has happened already, and what is going to happen until the unit is completed. All this helps the student to move from the last class and the last hall change into concentrating on the day's material at hand. Visuals can be extremely useful here to help the mind focus on the material. Many teachers find that with an extended time block, it is possible to move from material presentation to activities and projects that help make the material belong to the student. This can also enable concentration to deepen. Each of the sample lessons presented in this book follows the Inquire-Gather-Process-Apply sequence, which is most conducive to focus and is very brain compatible.

TIME TO ENGAGE THE LEARNER

The clue to engagement lies in varying what Caine and Caine (1991) call "states of arousal" so that interest and motivation can be sustained. While teachers may dislike the thought that the classroom could be entertaining, in order for engaged rigor to take place, some interest and attraction needs to occur. In addition, without a connection to real life, or the concerns the students bring to school, the content is boring, which is why teachers in block scheduling suggest the importance of a short activity that actually hooks the student into the material being covered. "There is more time to insert such 'hooking' activities in longer class periods" (Fitzgerald 1996, 20).

There is often such pressure in the traditional bell schedule that teachers feel the necessity to jump right in and get the material covered as quickly as possible. While this may serve the content and give the teacher a sense (if not the illusion) that the material is being covered, attention needs to be given to bringing the learner along. The biggest challenge for the teacher is to alter the instructional approaches so that students become engaged in choosing, directing, and fully participating in the learning process. Initially, this may seem overwhelming to the teacher accustomed to lecturing as the primary instructional strategy. Nevertheless, teachers, when confronted with the challenge of expanded time blocks, are making the effort to vary instructional approaches and create lessons that engage the learner.

The key to success in the block is using varied instructional strategies in the classroom, which relieves boredom and maintains focus and attention. "The more closely the students are involved with the information, the more likely it will stick with them. Through research projects, collaborative activities, oral presentations, use of technology, and critiquing of one another's work, students engage more actively in the topic at hand than when simply reading or listening" (Wyatt 1996, 16).

Although many teachers initially report that the shift to block scheduling takes a great deal of time and energy, they add quickly that the shift in their students' receptiveness to learning has made it all worthwhile. Brain-compatible learning is eminently engaging and when done well is rigorous and challenging, allowing students to pursue their greatest potential.

Engaged in Learning

Teachers need to concentrate not only on the content of a particular discipline but also amass a huge repertoire of effective teaching strategies, tools, and approaches. In this way, the teacher becomes more like an artist than ever before imagined. If the content is the idea in the head of a musician, then these strategies, tools, and approaches become more like the various instruments in the orchestra from among which the composer chooses to create a piece of music. The teacher then chooses which instrument will best convey the content, will best speak to the particular class, and will ultimately captivate the learners.

Enriched Learning Environment

Expanded time block scheduling is exactly the opportunity many teachers have been looking for to put into practice brain-compatible teaching approaches, which will do the job of blending content, skills, and processes. When content, skills, and processes are linked to many areas of the lives of the students, motivation for learning is enhanced.

In the past, the education system presumed that enough students would pick up high level thinking skills on their own. Those who didn't and who did poorly in school went on, if they were lucky, to find jobs in the unskilled job market. Today and tomorrow, every student will be in situations where more and more learning and relearning will be required. In the twenty-first century it is more important than ever before that upon graduation every student has the tools to become a skilled problem solver.

TIME TO TEACH CONTENT, SKILLS, AND PROCESSES

The call today is not just for students to dig deep into the content but also for them to develop skills and learn processes that will serve them on into adult life. Some teachers report that expanded block formats permit attention to skills and processes to occur while maintaining a focus on content. Students have the time not only to process material but also to learn how to learn, without de-emphasizing content. On the contrary, there is a great need to give students a grasp of skills and processes along with the content. The content is a tool that can be used not just for its own sake but to help uncover and/or foster student problem solving and processing skills. Content standards continue to evolve and change as new theories, technologies, and practices emerge. Emphasizing content to the exclusion of problem solving makes today's lesson obsolete by tomorrow. Students need to know how to continue learning, how to keep abreast of shifting and expanding

information, and how to attain learning skills and processes to help them focus on content.

The good news is that there are teachers and schools who are implementing instructional approaches that blend content, skills, and processes. Successful teachers employ brain-compatible learning strategies such as cooperative learning, thematic instruction, and multidisciplinary curriculum in conjunction with authentic assessment tools.

TIME TO IMPROVE THE SCHOOL CLIMATE

"Currently, the greatest support for block scheduling appears to be related to the overall improvement in school climate and the quality of the school day for both students and teachers"(Rettig and Canady 1996, 10). Teachers often comment that they recognize a dramatic positive shift in the entire school climate with the advent of extended time blocks. Such teachers confirm what Canady and Rettig suggest: The mere fact of fewer passing periods encourages fewer disruptions than would normally occur during frequent passing periods (Canady and Rettig 1993). The move from many passing periods to actually just one in the morning and one in the afternoon has had a definitive calming effect in the atmosphere of schools practicing the "4 by 4 Block" or the "Block 8." In addition, many teachers report that a longer class period has actually enabled many students to stay focused and involved in a way not possible with the constant change of the traditional bell schedule format. It is logical to extrapolate from this that short instructional periods can actually inhibit challenging learning environments. A block format can actually reduce stress in the teaching and learning day.

A World of Possibilities

As teachers become accustomed to an extended time format, they move away from their concern for how they are going to change their instruction and modify their content to working productively in a block format. They are then able to discern the tremendous possibilities for total change in the school climate that can occur as a result of well-implemented alternative scheduling. Creating a more relaxed and a more individually challenging environment can create a school where both teachers and students will *want* to be. Consequently, block scheduling has actually brought about a decrease in both student and staff absenteeism.

Meaning-filled Content

True learning is more than just skin deep. With the increasing volume of content material, teachers are in a bind. How can they enable their students to grasp all the necessary information while at the same time dealing with it in enough depth that students come away with lasting understanding and the ability to apply that understanding to new circumstances? The expanded time available to teachers and students in the block can be just the answer.

TIME TO DIG DEEP

There is a huge amount of content that students need to grasp not only to become familiar with a particular discipline but also to pass the standardized tests and the various college boards. On the other hand, employers are asking for employees who know how to think critically, how to problem solve, and how to continue learning on the job. Exposure to material alone does not guarantee that the material has been absorbed and retained. The core curriculum is becoming ever more demanding and the volume of material massive. Opportunities to make the connections, explore the meanings embedded in the material, and reflect upon and process the material are needed. Expanded time blocks can allow for significant amounts of material to be absorbed and worked with so that depth of understanding can emerge. Sadly, though perhaps not surprisingly, "much of the effort put into teaching and studying is wasted because students do not adequately process" (Caine and Caine 1991, 84). Time to connect meaning to the material through reflective and higher-order thinking processes moves that material into long-term accessible memory. Because of the advantage more time permits, access to long-term memory is increased. Brain-compatible learning in the context of an extended block schedule offers a chance for students to become genuine researchers and learners, which generates positive habits and skills that can continue into student lives beyond the final exam.

Processing the Practice

Processing and applying strategies may be practiced in the traditionally scheduled classroom; however, time does not allow for the presentation of learning to take place on the same day as the processing and application phases. When the processing and applying activities are presented on the following day, time must be spent going over the material presented the previous day before the processing and applying can begin. Time is actually saved when part of the longer periods is used to introduce material that is immediately followed by strategies and activities that help students process, reflect, understand, and then apply the material. The more time that elapses during which material is not processed and applied (even a span of twenty-four hours is significant), the more material can be forgotten or lost. Conversely, when material is immediately processed and applied (as is possible most times only in the context of an extended time block), students have a chance to immediately realize the importance and relevance of the content.

When time for reflection and active processing is allowed, actually more material is firmly established in the brain than when vast amounts of content are rapidly covered. Teachers are finding that longer time blocks offer a great flexibility and dynamic rhythm to instruction when a high intensity activity, such as team presentations, is followed by one of lower intensity, like journaling. (See the discussion of "pulsed learning" in chapter 4.)

TIME TO MAKE LEARNING CONNECTIONS

In a traditional scheduling context, subjects and curricula are discrete, fragmented pieces, which communicates to students that the world is just as fragmented and disorganized. The reality is "Everything is connected to everything else," as Robert Sylwester asserts (1995, 140). While Sylwester is talking about the way human brain cells and sections are interconnected, it is also true about the world teachers and students inhabit. Students are done a disservice when connections are not facilitated. Teachers in the block have an enhanced opportunity to help students perceive the implicit connection between concepts. Conveying the big picture is difficult in traditional scheduling, and relating material to other disciplines is even more difficult.

A related concern is finding the schedule that allows the teacher to guide students to make the kind of intellectual and practical connections that well-presented material can foster in the classroom. The time spent enabling students to make such connections results in more lively participation and deeper motivation on the part of the students. Teachers themselves report experiencing elevated morale and renewed motivation when working with extended time blocks.

Fostering Connections

Reflective questions can start the connections cooking in the minds of the students. Many times teachers feel they can only ask these kinds of questions at the end of the lesson, at the end of the class period, or at the end of the unit. Instead, these connection-generating questions can be used throughout the time block and throughout the lesson. As the research is suggesting, the more connections get made, the more real learning occurs.

Examples of reflective questions teachers may pose include the following:

- What does the concept of _____ remind you of?
- Where have you heard something like this before?
- How does this remind you of something we worked on last semester?
- How could you apply this concept we've discovered in history to science, math, or language arts?
- In what ways have you encountered this principle in your daily life?

The attend-experience-reflect circuit of each phase of the Four-Phase Lesson Plan offers a built-in opportunity for ongoing reflection.

Alternative Scheduling Formats

In 1996, eminent block scheduling researchers Michael Rettig and Robert Lynn Canady reported that more than 50 percent of high schools in the United States were using or thinking about using some form of extended time blocks. In a separate study the same year Sadowski found that after the first year or two of adjustment, 80 percent of both students and teachers taking part in alternative scheduling prefer the extended time blocks over traditional scheduling.

Block scheduling can take many forms, but the following represent those most widely used. It's important to keep in mind, however, that the key to alternative scheduling is to find and modify a schedule type that best suits the particular school environment and population it is to serve.

Block 8 Plan

Some schools hold four classes one day, alternating with four different classes the next day. Such schedules are sometimes referred to as "Block 8" (also called the Alternating, or the A/B, Plan) and maintain the advantage of longer class times while enabling teachers to meet regularly with students all year long (see Figure 2.3). Consequently, the Block 8 avoids some of the sequential gaps in math and foreign language course studies that concern many people with the 4 by 4 discussed next. Many schools involved in block scheduling use the Block 8 plan. It seems that teachers can buy into the Block 8 more readily than other plans because it allows them to see the student all year long and eliminates potential sequential gaps in instruction. Highly sequential subjects such as foreign language and mathematics may be best taught continually throughout the year without taking a semester or session off between classes. The Block 8 also reduces the apprehension some persons have relative to student performance on standardized tests. The concern has been that material learned in the fall will not be retained by the time the spring standardized tests come around.

In any given day, students only need to focus on four classes. Many students report that they like the choice of when to complete their homework for the next class meeting—they can decide to do it the first or second evening after it has been assigned.

Block 8 Schedule

Monday	Tuesday	Wednesday	Thursday	Friday
Class 1	Class 5	Class 1	Class 5	Class 1
Class 2	Class 6	Class 2	Class 6	Class 2
Lunch	Lunch	Lunch	Lunch	Lunch
Class 3	Class 7	Class 3	Class 7	Class 3
Class 4	Class 8	Class 4	Class 8	Class 4

Figure 2.3

4 by 4 Block Plan

In what is also called "an accelerated" or "Block 4" plan, some schools hold the same four classes every day, completing an entire year's course in a semester. The following semester these schools hold four different classes, also completed in a semester (see Figure 2.4). What teachers like about such a plan is the opportunity to have only ninety students at a time (as opposed to 150 or more). Students also benefit from teachers having fewer students. It is far more likely that a teacher will get to know ninety students per semester well than would be possible with 150, resulting in a potentially much deeper student-teacher connection. Such connections have been shown to mitigate students' tuning out or dropping out. Teachers also have the advantage of concentrating their energies on only three classes per semester. The remaining ninety minutes a day is left for the substantial planning brain-compatible instructional strategies require.

4 by 4 Schedule				
Monday	**Tuesday**	**Wednesday**	**Thursday**	**Friday**
Class 1 90 min.	Class 1 90 min.	Class 1 90 min.	Class 1 90 min.	Class 1 90 min.
Class 2 90 min.	Class 2 90 min.	Class 2 90 min.	Class 2 90 min.	Class 2 90 min.
Lunch 30 min.	Lunch 30 min.	Lunch 30 min.	Lunch 30 min.	Lunch 30 min.
Class 3 90 min.	Class 3 90 min.	Class 3 90 min.	Class 3 90 min.	Class 3 90 min.
Class 4 90 min.	Class 4 9 0 min.	Class 4 90 min.	Class 4 90 min.	Class 4 90 min.

Figure 2.4

The Copernican Plan

The Copernican model was named by its innovator, Joseph M. Carroll, for the 16th-century scholar Nicolaus Copernicus, who revolutionized thinking during the Middle Ages with his notion of the movements of the planets around the sun rather than vice versa. At its inception, this scheduling model may have seemed as revolutionary. It combines longer blocks of time (in ninety-minute, two-hour, or four-hour partitions—called "macroclasses") with smaller blocks of time in an extremely varied and flexible schedule. This model has tremendous advantages in terms of flexibility. When the schedule is done well, it allows students to get the classes they want at some point during their time in school. The Copernican plan, however, is complex (see Figure 2.5). Schedulers might find it a bit more challenging than they bargained for until they gain experience with it. Some educators have found that this plan is too complex to be efficiently implemented in a middle school environment.

The Copernican Schedule	
Possible Day A	**Possible Day B**
Class 1 — All Morning for 30 Days	Class 1 — ¹/₂ Morning for 60 Days
	Class 2 — ¹/₂ Morning for 60 Days
Class 2 — Music/Art 70 Minutes & LUNCH 35 Minutes	LUNCH 35 Minutes & Class 3 — Music/Art 70 Minutes
Class 3 Seminar or PE/Study/Help	Class 4 Seminar or PE/Study/Help

Figure 2.5

The School Calendar

Modified instructional terms can produce more time for learning. Seventy-five-day terms in conjunction with interim, or mini-terms, of fifteen days are one way to alter the school calendar. Intensive short courses taught during the interim terms can include enrichment, remediation, or structured review for college board or advanced placement tests, among other subjects. (See Sample Four-Phase Lesson # 5: *Who Framed Sir Isaac Newton* for an example of structured review.) The fifteen-day (or three-week) term can also be used for rotating teaching assignments with staff development courses. Moving from semesters to trimesters and year-round schools can also allow for greater flexibility in scheduling (Cushman 1995).

Before- and after-school workshops, seminars, explorations, tutoring sessions, and service learning projects have found their way formally and informally onto school schedules with increased regularity. It seems obvious that to maintain or enhance the richness of the educational experience in or out of the block, some alteration of the school day (and even the school year) is close at hand (National Education Commission 1994).

Finally, moving to an alternative scheduling is not a magic wand that once waved over the system will automatically bring about the desired result. However, "by partitioning the school day into larger chunks of time, by looking at the concept of flexible, modular scheduling that accommodates learning, school faculties create a framework that favors the needs of the learner" (Fogarty 1996, *v*).

Sample Four-Phase Lesson # 2, like each of the lessons shown here, exemplifies the best practice in a block setting by making the most of the time at hand. It is a middle school language arts lesson on the book *To Kill a Mockingbird* and deals with the impact of prejudice on justice. Notice the use of visuals to reinforce students' understanding of complex issues and concepts. Some of the skills developed and practiced include improving as reading and synthesizing information, recognizing bias in writing and speaking, writing a persuasive argument, debating issues, and improving critical thinking—the careful analysis of qualities and an evaluation of their comparative worth. Other topics that may be selected for this lesson include the exploration of such topics or issues as jury dynamics, human relationships, historical fiction as a genre, bigotry, tolerance, ethically principled behavior, and civil disobedience. The curriculum integration is language arts with civics and technology.

Sample Four-Phase Lesson Plan

Sample Lesson 2

Can Prejudice Kill a Mockingbird?

Level: Middle

Curriculum Integration: Language Arts, Civics, and Technology

Multiple Intelligences

- ❏ Bodily/Kinesthetic
- ☑ Interpersonal
- ☑ Intrapersonal
- ☑ Logical/Mathematical
- ❏ Musical
- ❏ Naturalist
- ☑ Verbal/Linguistic
- ☑ Visual/Spatial

Content Standards

LANGUAGE ARTS
Demonstrates competence in general skills and strategies for reading a variety of literary texts

CIVICS
Understands issues concerning the disparities between ideals and reality in American political and social life

TECHNOLOGY
Evaluates electronic sources of information
Uses the Internet to communicate and "publish" original material

INQUIRE PHASE
25 MINUTES

Inquire Activity Option A
Objective: Students define terms related to prejudice, justice, and bias.

ATTEND

Students write their responses to the following metacognitive questions regarding bias, prejudice, and justice in their personal metacognitive journals.

- What does the word *bias* mean to you?
- What are some of your biases?
- What does the word *prejudice* mean to you?
- When have you acted prejudiced? Why?
- When did someone act prejudiced against you? What happened?
- Is "justice for all" a myth? Is it possible to attain? Under what conditions/circumstances is it possible?
- How is the quality of justice related to bias and prejudice?
- On a scale from one to ten (one being completely unjust and ten being absolutely fair and equitable) how would you rate yourself? What circumstances can or have had an impact on how fair you are?

EXPERIENCE: "MIX AND MATCH"

Early on in the unit, students were instructed to create an index card for each character they encountered and every incident they felt was significant in *To Kill a Mockingbird*. (The cards could have also been used to study the plot of the novel in a previous lesson.)

Students . . .

- Form groups of four and select a "secretary."
- As a class and guided by the teacher, create definitions for the following words:

bias	intolerance	racism
bigotry	justice	stereotype
ethics	morality	tolerance
injustice	prejudice	

Each secretary . . .

- Records the collective definitions on index cards for his or her group.

Students...

- Working in their small groups recall or cite a specific incident from the book that represents or depicts each of the eleven vocabulary words. (There may be more than one character or incident per word.)

The teacher . . .
- Debriefs each group by leading a brief discussion of the examples students identified.

Inquire Activity Option B

Objective: Students create a graphic organizer analogy chart.

ATTEND

The teacher directs student attention to a quote by Victor Hugo by asking the students to . . .
- Look for the images Victor Hugo uses to express universal problems of prejudice.
- Think about how Hugo might define prejudice.
- Imagine a simile that illustrates your definition of bias.

EXPERIENCE: "HAUNTED BY PREJUDICE"

Superstition, bigotry and prejudice, ghosts though they are, cling tenaciously to life; they are shades armed with tooth and claw. They must be grappled with unceasingly, for it is a fateful part of human destiny that it is condemned to wage perpetual war against ghosts.

—Victor Hugo from *Les Miserable* (1862)

The teacher . . .
- Models how to create the analogy chart using the Hugo quote.
- Asks students to identify three supporting reasons for Hugo's analogy. (Figure 2.6 provides an example.)

Prejudice is like a ghost because:
1. You can feel it, you know that it exists, but you can't touch or see it
2. The ghost's purpose is to frighten, haunt, and make life miserable
3. Ghost persists

Figure 2.6

The teacher . . .

• Assigns students to groups of three or four and instructs them to create an analogy chart of the word *bias* or *prejudice*.

Analogy Chart

Prejudice is like a _____.
Because: (Include at least three supporting reasons for your comparison) 1.) 2.) 3.)
Draw a visual representation of the simile you created above.

Figure 2.7

Students . . .

• In the same small groups create their own analogies of prejudice.
• Share their analogies with the whole class.
• Post their analogies on the wall.

REFLECT

The teacher asks the following questions:

• What similarities did you notice among the various analogies? Differences?
• What has changed in your definition of *bias* and *prejudice*?
• How might you identify bias or prejudice in yourself and others?

GATHER PHASE
25 MINUTES

Gather Activity

Objective: Students create a Venn Diagram comparing characters' personalities or actions.

ATTEND

The teacher focuses student attention on the next task by asking the following questions . . .

- Do you recall what a Venn diagram looks like? (The teacher draw two intersecting circles on the board or chart paper.)
- What are Venn diagrams used to illustrate? (The teacher refreshes student memories about using Venn Diagrams—see chapter 4.)
- Do you believe the adage that "actions speak louder than words"? Why or why not?

EXPERIENCE: "CHARACTER COMMONALITY"

Students . . .

- Working with a partner or independently, use a Venn diagram to compare/contrast elements in the novel *To Kill a Mockingbird* that show bias or prejudice. (A diagram considered "advanced and sophisticated" demonstrates creativity with the shape of the Venn Diagram—a girl's head overlapping a boy's head or a dog's head with a man's head—and compares more than two characters on one diagram. See Figure 2.8 "Rubric for Venn diagram.")

Rubric for Venn Diagram

Qualities Evaluated	Not Yet (1)	Emerging Understanding (2)	Accomplished Work (3)	Advanced and Sophisticated Work (4)
Diagram Design	Unevenly drawn from circles	Two intersecting circles neatly drawn	Intersecting figures/shapes other than circles	Very unique and creative intersecting figures and/or more than two intersecting figures
Points of Comparison (area of intersection)	2 or 3 superficial points of comparison	4 or 5 basic points	6 to 7 points that evidence understanding of novel's characters	more than 7 points that evidence a synthesis of character traits and actions and the themes of justice and prejudice
Points of Contrast	superficial details in unequal in number for each character	an equal number of physical characteristics for each character	at least 8 total attributes showing both physical and internal elements characteristics	at least nine total attributes that evidences deep understanding and a unique and informed point of view
Accuracy of Information	seems to misunderstand relationships between characters	some inaccuracies or not supported by the reading or student presentation	all points were accurate	all points were accurate and relied upon a combination of information.

Figure 2.8

- Choose one of the following character pairings:
    - (a) Scout with Jem
    - (b) Arthur "Boo" Radley with Tom Robinson
    - (c) The Cunningham family with the Finch family
    - (d) Poor "black folks" with poor "white folks"
    - (e) Rabid dog with Mr. Robert E. Lee Ewell (Mayella's father)
    - (f) Mayella Violet Ewell with Calpurnia (the Finch's housekeeper)
    - (g) two or more other characters of student's choice

- Share their Venn Diagrams with the class.
- Post their diagrams on the wall after they present them.

REFLECT

The teacher . . .

- Asks students to revisit the entries they made in their metacognitive journals in the inquire phase of the lesson and revise their answers where necessary.

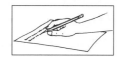

PROCESS PHASE
25 MINUTES

Process Activity

Objective: Students engage in a debate on prejudices then and now.

ATTEND

The teacher . . .

- Posts the following quote:

  Thinking is what a great many people think they are doing when they are merely rearranging their prejudices.

  —William James, *The Will to Believe*

- Asks the students the following as part of a class discussion. . .
  - Describe a time when you observed or heard about someone doing exactly what the quote describes.
  - How can a debate be useful in generating new thoughts not just rearranging or reinforcing prejudices?
  - How should you prepare for a debate?

EXPERIENCE: "RELATE THROUGH DEBATE"

The teacher . . .

- Posts the following statement:
  Students today are less prejudiced than students living in the 1930s.
- Divides students into groups of three or four persons and randomly assigns one group to the affirmative position or to the negative position.

Students . . .

- Identify four key points in their small groups, to support their assigned positions.
- Engage in the debate by alternating statements supporting the affirmative side with statements supporting the negative side.
- Support their positions by citing personal examples, points raised in the novel, or information they have studied.

The teacher . . .

- Moderates the debate by calling on both sides and recording the main points raised on the board or chart paper.
- Facilitates a brief discussion at the end of the debate to help students decide, by vote, which two points are most convincing for both sides.

REFLECT

Teacher poses the following reflection questions as student pairs discuss them . . .

- What position do you personally support—affirmative or negative?
- Did you change your position during the debate? If so, what influenced your thinking?
- How can listening to opposing sides of an issue help you minimize the effect of your biases and prejudices on your thinking?
- What do you think it takes to change someone's bias or prejudice?

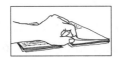

APPLY PHASE
15 MINUTES

Apply Activity

Objective: Students prepare a survey, write interview questions, or formulate questions for a later visit to a Web site to determine others' opinions regarding bias and prejudice.

Students . . .

- Form groups of three or four persons based on which of the following projects each would like to undertake:

Project A:

Prepare a survey to determine the attitudes, biases, or prejudices of class-mates on one of the following topics:

- Race and intelligence
- Family annual income and popularity
- Most respected professions
- Good looks and leadership
- GPA and common sense
- Athletics and preferential treatment
- Other relevant topic okayed by the teacher

Project B:

Prepare interview questions to assess the opinions, prejudices, or perceived biases of two or three adults, a combination of female and male respondents, in school or out in the community, on the following issues:

- Working women and the "glass ceiling" in education, business, and government
- White males and reverse discrimination
- Minority worker wages and job opportunities
- Violence and the media
- Other acceptable topic approved by the teacher

Project C:

Prepare to visit a Web site(s) reviewed by the teacher (see Appendix) and participate in a discussion or chat group or post questions regarding the themes of honor, prejudice, and justice as they compare in 1930s America and America today.

REFLECT

The teacher . . .

- Posts the following quote:

  Injustice anywhere is a threat to justice everywhere.
  —Martin Luther King, Jr. from "Letter from Birmingham Jail"

- Asks the following questions as part of a class discussion:
  - What condition or conditions prompted Dr. King to make this state-ment?
  - How can injustice to someone on the other side of the country impact justice in your community?
  - In the novel *To Kill a Mockingbird*, how could the injustice Tom Robinson faced impact justice for the Finch family?
  - How has/does injustice to another person impact either directly or indirectly on your family?

CHAPTER 3

CONTENT AND CURRICULUM

Curriculum is the heart of why we do what we do as teachers and what we leave as our legacy to the next generation.

—Susan Kovalik 1997

Duck or Cover?

Perhaps one of the most exciting aspects of moving to, or even considering, block scheduling is that it stimulates dialogue about prioritizing curricular content. As is becoming increasingly clear, it is necessary to balance the massive amounts of content prescribed by forty-nine states, thirteen of the national subject-area associations, and district mandates with the instructional time available to present it. More and more curriculum is being added, causing many teachers to feel they are drowning in a sea of information (Chapman 1993). Numerous school systems burden teachers with the untenable notion that "covering" vast amounts of material is the only way to prepare students to score well on the standardized tests and entrance examinations that ensure their respective academic futures. (See chapter 5 for an in-depth discussion of assessment, achievement, and testing in the block.) A profound realignment of the conventional paradigm is needed—from one in which content is "covered" to one in which students are given the time and tools to draw their own meaning from the material. While teachers may not cover as much content after such an adjustment, the content that is covered is really the students' own material in a way not previously occurring. "By covering less content but learning it better, students in the long run have an overall greater level of mastery" (Wyatt 1996, 17). Students are then better prepared for lifelong learning instead of just for the next big test.

Ultimately, educators are left with three options: increase instructional time, decrease the breadth of the content in favor of more depth, or integrate content area study to address multiple content standards simultaneously.

As discussed in chapter 2, multiple class changes per day deeply cut into instructional time, as does time spent reviewing material presented the previous day. Moving to a block schedule can actually provide more time for learning within the confines of the conventional six-and-one-half-hour school day. Extending the school day or school year and eliminating electives from the course offerings are perhaps some of the most controversial ideas for creating more time.

Priorities: Quality Versus Quantity

Robert J. Marzano and John S. Kendall (1998) of the Mid-Continent Regional Educational Laboratory have identified, after an inventory of the 116 documents constructed by thirteen subject-area associations, "200 separate standards that address 3,093 more specific topics, commonly referred to as benchmarks" for grades K through 12. They have extrapolated from this number and the average number of days per year that a student attends school in the United States (180) that conventional instruction in this content would require twenty-one years of education (eight more than the thirteen years students now attend). In addition, the core curriculum is more demanding than ever. At the same time, mandates have added additional material to be covered: contemporary health topics, conflict management, violence prevention, and other subjects. Teachers are being called upon to make choices in what they teach and how they teach to make the most of the allotted time.

As illustrated in Figure 3.1 "Prioritizing Curriculum in the Block," selective abandonment, jigsawing, graphic organizers, curriculum frameworks, curriculum mapping, and curriculum integration are ways that teachers can confidently prioritize curricular content.

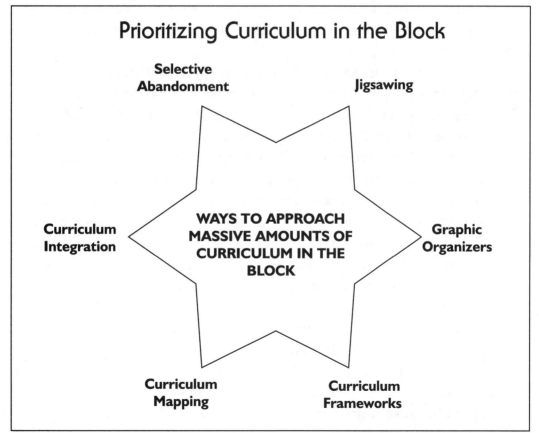

Figure 3.1

Selective Abandonment

What can a teacher do to help students work smarter, not harder, in the flood of information? One answer, suggested by Arthur Costa (1999), is the *selective abandonment* of portions of content. Carefully and thoughtfully selected content can be cut without negatively impacting student learning. In fact, pruned content often results in fuller student understanding. Selective abandonment, or streamlining the curriculum, calls for serious examination of the curriculum and deciding what to keep and what to leave out.

Marzano and Kendall (1998) suggest that school districts survey local community members and organizations to determine what content standards, and which benchmarks for attaining those standards, are priorities to that particular community or district. They contend that a grassroots local approach to identify standards would be able to do what the subject-matter experts could not: identify a workable set of standards in terms of their practical application. Such an approach would indeed involve the community substantially but may not be palatable to some educational professionals. A more realistic model would be for teachers to take the data derived from the completed surveys and use that to influence team decisions on curriculum and content.

On the other hand, Rettig and Canady (1996) assert that defining curricular priorities is the role and responsibility of the teacher. The expertise of the teacher is needed to discern what is absolutely crucial for the student versus what can be eliminated or lightly acknowledged. Because of the immensity and difficulty of this task, it is most appropriate for departments or teams of teachers to work together. Many perspectives generate a more balanced result than that of only one teacher working on a course alone. The first step for teacher teams in this process is to ask the following questions in relation to potential course material:

- What is the essential concept?
- What content material best facilitates the understanding of what is essential?
- What activities employing what teaching tools are most appropriate?
- What are the essential concepts and standards?

The specific criteria set forth in Figure 3.2 can be used to make decisions about which material to incorporate into lesson and unit plans. Potential topics can be tested to see into which of three categories they might fall: Essential, Supportive, or Extraneous.

Selective Abandonment Criteria

Essential
- Has a real-life practical application
- Fundamental step in a larger process
- Based in the present
- Helps students function in the world in which they live
- District- or system-articulated benchmark directly tied to a vital concept

Supportive
- Collaterally linked to a curricular objective
- Promotes independent study opportunity
- Can be more fully developed in another curricular area
- Provokes student interest and motivation to "learn more"
- Provides additional opportunities for students to develop a wide range of intelligences

Extraneous
- Based in knowledge about theory or the past without practical application in the future or present
- Fun but not linked to a curricular concept
- Exercises only the logical/mathematical and verbal/linguistic intelligences
- Doesn't promote positive group interdependence

Figure 3.2

ESSENTIAL

Curriculum items in this category are deemed absolutely necessary by the practitioner(s) for the knowledge base of the student. This category looks to the future. It raises the question of what students will need ten, fifteen, and twenty-five years from now on their journey of lifelong learning. This category also keeps an eye on the standardized tests and includes information that the teacher knows from experience will be included on examinations of this kind.

SUPPORTIVE

This category includes material that can be covered in passing or touched upon lightly. It may be a simple concept or an event that needs a brief reference and might also include material that could be divided, studied, and shared by student teams in a class "jigsaw" strategy.

EXTRANEOUS

Such material is not unimportant; it may actually be useful and helpful. However, when compared with other material, it is not *as* helpful or not *as* useful.

Content Delivery Structures

Many critics of block scheduling are deeply concerned that there is less emphasis on crucial facts and information because in some situations there will be fewer minutes spent in class than in traditional schedules. They would go so far as to talk about the "dumbing down" of curriculum (Rettig and Canady 1996). Precisely the opposite can occur. Although a traditional class may "cover" nine chapters over the course of a semester, static instructional techniques coupled with the brusqueness of the bell schedule may actually cause students to retain only about five chapters worth of meaning because they have not had the time or experiences necessary to make the material part of long-term memory. On the other hand, when only seven chapters are presented using brain-compatible pedagogy, the students may full well be able to grasp and internalize six-and-one-half chapters worth of meaning, resulting in a net gain of a chapter and one half over the traditional schedule. This is, of course, an oversimplification, but it does help make clear that the streamlined curriculum as taught in an extended time format is not a digest or abbreviation and most certainly is not a "dumbing down."

Jigsawing

There are a huge number of cooperative learning strategies, but the focus here is on those that pertain to the issue of curriculum in block scheduling. A commonly used strategy in cooperative learning has been called jigsawing. David Johnson and Roger Johnson (1986) outline this strategy in detail in their book *Circles of Learning*. Material to be studied is divided either among members of a group who then teach it to other group members, or among groups in the class, who then present it to the whole class.

The benefits of the jigsaw technique are several. Most importantly, it can be used in that essential first step of gathering a lot of information and evaluating that information for key insights or critical points. It is only a preliminary step, not a processing or culminating step, which is why it is best used in the gather phase of a Four-Phase lesson plan. The technique allows students to organize the information they reviewed into words and phrases that make sense to them in order to share the information with other students. Jigsawing is also helpful in reducing the amount of reading or data gathering that might be daunting or overwhelming for some student. The use of expert groups also allows students to have ownership of the information and feel a sense of responsibility to share that information with other students.

Teachers can use jigsawing as a means of...

- introducing students to concepts
- requiring students to become teachers
- teaching students how to read information, synthesize key points, and explain the information to others
- providing students with a learning technique of reading information first for concepts and then returning to it for more details and specifics.

Jigsawing doesn't works for all situations, however, particularly if the information is sequential and each part is necessary to understand the subsequent parts of the material, for instance studying the periodic table in chemistry. As with any cooperative learning strategy, jigsawing requires clear group roles and precise instructions for what the process and the product need to be. Choosing the material strategically and then passing it out to cooperative learning groups to study and then present to the whole class is one way to get a class familiar with a body of material.

Graphic Organizers

Another commonly used strategy in cooperative learning is the application of graphic organizers. Graphic organizers are visual tools that help students organize and process a great deal of information. They are sometimes called cognitive maps, visual displays, or advance organizers. Graphic organizers can help to make relationships and connections visible or concrete for students. Sometimes they even reveal what students are thinking or even *how* students are thinking. These visual tools can help launch the student into a writing assignment, a project, a debate, a role-play skit, or many other activities. (See chapter 4 for a full discussion of the types and uses of graphic organizers.)

Curricular Frameworks

A curricular framework, or curriculum model, is the way a curriculum unit is organized, while instructional strategies (discussed in chapter 4) are ways the material can be presented. The curriculum frameworks are project-oriented curricula, thematic units, performance-based learning, problem-based learning, service learning, and case studies. Brain-compatible learning recognizes that various disciplines relate common information for the brain to recognize and organize. Teachers need to look at the entire course to be taught (the whole semester, trimester, or mini session) and then plan out how and where they can use these curriculum frameworks. Such organizing structures can help to connect several disciplines together. Resultant interconnections can even shorten curriculum time, as similar material is taught only once instead of over and over in different curriculum disciplines. Students are then able to experience relationships and see the real-life connections and applications to material being taught.

The concept of civil rights can encompass:
- The civil rights movement of the 1960s
- African-American history
- Gandhi's nonviolent resistance movement in India
- Thoreau's treatise on civil disobedience
- Protest literature
- Current events issues such as gender-based discrimination
- Recent African struggles
- Songs and art that embody the civil rights theme

In the above example, the disciplines of history, social studies, civics, languages arts, art, and music, are all linked proving a curricular framework is a powerful tool. Such sophisticated teaching takes work as does anything worthwhile. Planning and communicating time for teachers is essential to success. Most block scheduling plans allow for ninety minutes or more of teacher planning per day, far in excess of the measly forty-five to fifty minutes provided for in the traditional structure. The classroom that incorporates interdisciplinary themes and connecting concepts requires a cooperation and connection among teaching staff that the very structure of the classroom and the school day has hindered up until now. Further, rigid, inflexible time schedules and the traditional isolation of teachers, perhaps especially high school teachers, have permitted very few connections among those teaching in similar disciplines, let alone among teachers of totally different disciplines. Block scheduling may catalyze new connections among the staff that will genuinely help to make content material more relevant to how students experience real life.

Many teachers are discovering ways to link disciplines together and save time while enriching the educational experience in the process. It is much more lifelike and brain-compatible to present material in as connected a way as it occurs in everyday life. "Students don't often see the connections among separate and distinct subjects....We need holistic ways to present information and get students involved in learning so they can apply what they've learned to their lives" (Fogarty and Stoehr 1995, 21).

The following six curricular frameworks illustrate some of the ways a unit can be structured to promote meaningful learning:

PROJECT-ORIENTED CURRICULA

Projects focus the curriculum and the learning around actually creating and making something to demonstrate the learning. Examples include:

- Social Studies—a project on a continent or a country could call for the creation of a travel brochure.
- Language Arts—a student might construct a model of a house in which a story takes place, making sure that the model accurately reflects the details the author included.
- Algebra—a student could create models of various curves that visually represent their equations.
- Physics—a student could construct various weights and pulleys or electronic circuitry.

Note that all of the above examples involve very hands-on projects that call for authentic demonstration of knowledge and learning. A block format permits time for the teacher to present the material followed by time for the students to work on the projects.

THEMATIC UNITS

A rethinking of the common practice of isolating content area curricula is called for. Such isolation is antithetical to how everyone experiences life. There are other ways to organize information than by placing it in discrete categories like language arts, algebra, chemistry, social studies, music, and physical education. A better way, a more brain-compatible way, is to organize curricular concepts around themes or issues such as

LIFE
- Birth
- Freedom
- Relationships
- Patterns
- Careers
- Travel
- The Shrinking Globe
- Entertainment
- Heroes and Heroines

GLOBAL CHALLENGES
- Polluted Environment
- Racism
- Genocide
- Hunger
- Shrinking Natural Resources
- War
- Fragmented Families
- Forced Migration of Peoples

Figure 3.3 "Circles Make the World Go 'Round" illustrates the way in which the sample lesson plan *Circles and Cycles*, found at the end of this chapter, works into a thematic unit.

If one chose to, the material in every content area could be taught in such a way. In time, with more communication among the teaching staff, teachers will discover more and more opportunities. Ninety minutes of planning time a day (available in the 4 by 4 Plan) or every other day (in a Block 8 Plan) allows for at least occasional meetings among staff who want to explore themes and connecting concepts.

A theme could be developed among various content areas or just within a teacher's own content discipline. It is the intent of thematic units to create themes that will grab the interest of students and teachers. Thematic units encourage teachers to prioritize and order content and precisely define directions for students. Students can do research based on the theme to construct a paper or a cooperative team presentation or project. An extended time format allows the students time to do some of the research within class time, but many students immersed in thematic instruction will continue their process of discovery beyond the class time.

Circles Make the World Go 'Round

Social Studies
Traditions
Use of rings
Transportation
Amusement Parks

Art/Music
Circle of Life, *The Lion King*
Circles in Nature
Records, tapes, CDs
Musical Instruments
Shapes of plants and animals

Math
Circumference, diameter, radius, radians, 0 to 360 degrees, angular/circular motion

CIRCLES
Make the World
Go 'Round

PE
Racing Tracks
Balls, bats, and bases
Dance
Joints and Levers
Choreography

Literature
Tolkein: *Lord of the Rings*
Knots on a Counting Rope
Bee Tree
Red Fern
The Giving Tree

Science
Simple Machines:
(pulleys, levers, bikes, wheelbarrows)
Fluid Dynamics
Pipes, bottles, hoses

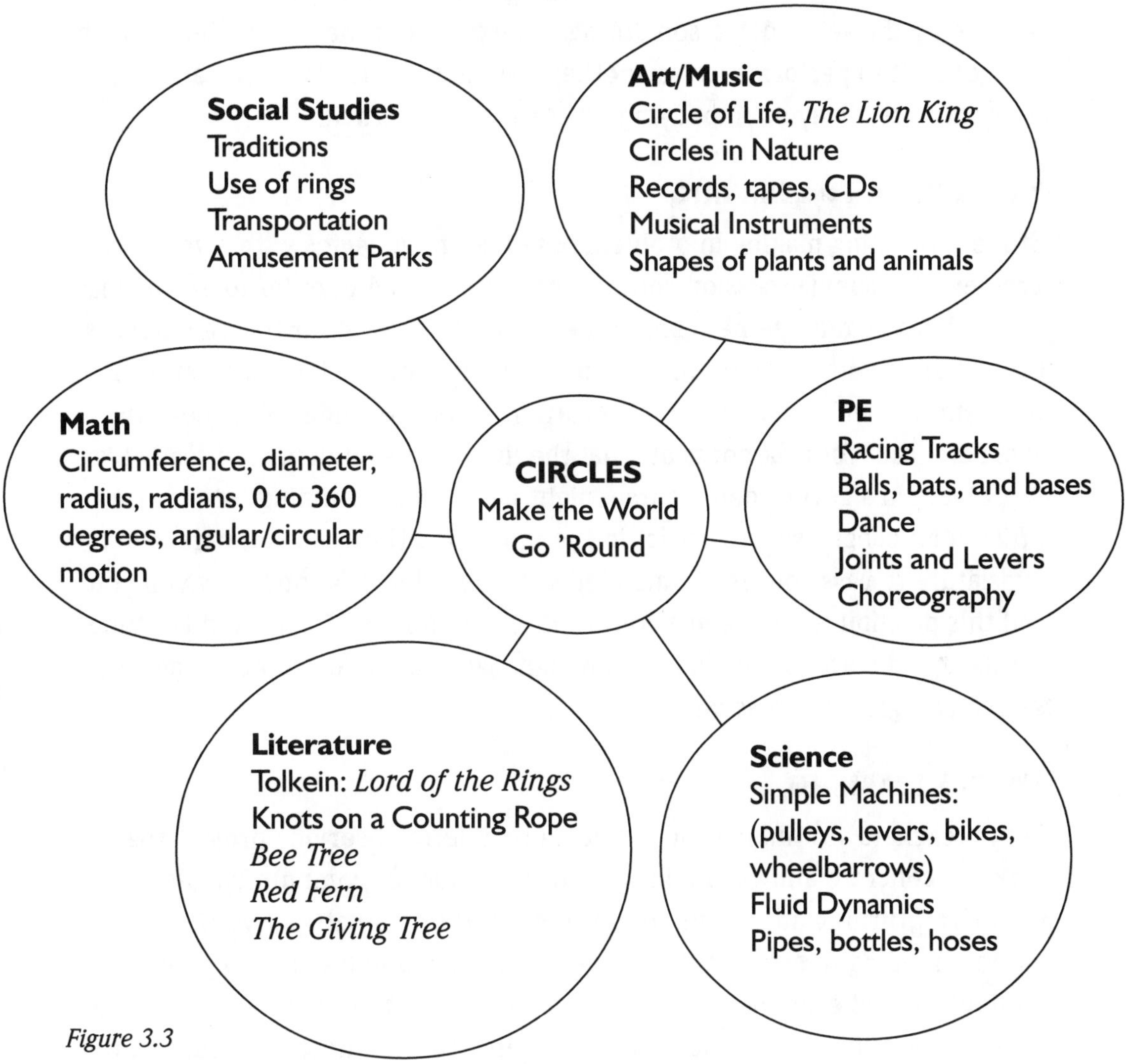

Figure 3.3

PERFORMANCE-BASED LEARNING

Performances involve some authentic execution. Musical, dance, and dramatic performances are perhaps obvious, but others can include:

- rewriting and performing a scene with a different spin from a Shakespearean play

- demonstrating a laboratory experiment
- showing a correct wrestling move
- cooking regional or traditional dishes
- acting out a skit in a foreign language

In each of these examples the students demonstrate what they have learned by the act of doing something. An extended time format demands this kind of shift to performance as another way to vary the class time and permits this direct way of embodying what has been learned.

PROBLEM-BASED LEARNING

Student meaning making in problem-based learning begins with a very messy problem or issue. Discussion and research are needed in order to grasp what the real problem might be. Then more research is called for before students can come up with some solutions. The challenge for teachers is creating a problem that will genuinely grab the attention of the students in the classroom and calls for awareness of what the lives of the students are really like. A problem in a government course might be: "You are running for political office for a congressional district in the inner city. How will you persuade the legislature to pass your recommended gun control legislation? How will you sell this position to the people you want to vote for you?" An extended time format again permits the students enough class time to do some of the research and group discussion.

SERVICE LEARNING

Some teachers are linking the curricula to a defined service project that makes a concrete and visible impact in the school or community. Cleaning up a river, turning an unsightly plot of ground into an attractive flower garden, reading to senior citizens, peer teaching, and mentoring younger students are all examples of service projects. It is important for the teacher to make sure that the service project is genuinely connected to curriculum content, standards, and/or benchmarks and also based on real needs. Because many of these service projects are carried out within class time, extended time formats allow for these beautifully. Service learning can have very positive and lasting influences on students' standards of conduct, attitudes, and understanding of course content.

CASE STUDIES

The use of a dramatic and compelling narrative is the kick-off for a particular unit of study. The narrative raises the concept or issue in a way that grabs the emotions of the students. Then through discussion and further research the students come to some resolution or position relative to the concept or issue. Again the case study could raise an issue as complex and deep as racism or as personal as lying. A math class could use an issue in a case study as a springboard for studying statistics or graphs. A chemistry class could use an issue in a case study to delve into environmental pollution. An extended time format permits the research time and cooperative group dialogue time that is not impossible but much more difficult in more traditional time formats.

Each of the six frameworks discussed provide ingenious ways of hooking the student into participating in the learning experience. Each finds a way to grab the student both in the intellect and in the emotions, at once building upon and sparking student motivation. When these approaches are presented well, the student ends up doing far more work than a teacher ever thought possible. Curricular frameworks can help create a genuine community of learners in the school environment.

Again, the more teacher teams collaborate in talking these through, the more winning insights can be gleaned relative to how such frameworks are carried out in the classroom. The nature of student involvement, the research tasks implied with each model, and finally the demand for teamwork requires more time than forty to fifty minutes.

Curriculum Mapping

Heidi Hayes Jacobs (1997) developed curriculum mapping as a way to help teachers get a hold of what other teachers are doing and to help them grasp what they themselves are doing in the classroom. If one were to imagine a huge matrix, across the top one would lay out the months of the school year or semester and down the left side would be categories such as particular curriculum units, needed skills, projects, guidelines and objectives, etc. (see Figure 3.4). After teachers fill out the matrices, they share their "curriculum maps" with other teachers. "Not only did people find the calendar an honest vehicle for communication about the curriculum, but they reported it was far more efficient than reading through lists of curriculum guidelines from other

Curriculum Mapping

Course_____ Instructor_____

	AUGUST	SEPTEMBER	OCTOBER	NOVEMBER	DECEMBER	JANUARY
CONTENT						
SKILLS						
ASSESSMENT						
STANDARDS						

Course_____ Instructor_____

	JANUARY	FEBRUARY	MARCH	APRIL	MAY	JUNE
CONTENT						
SKILLS						
ASSESSMENT						
STANDARDS						

Figure 3.4

departments" (Hayes Jacobs 1997, 2). Though it seems too simple to work, its very simplicity is the reason why it works. "Curriculum mapping amplifies the possibilities for long-range planning, short-term preparation, and clear communication" (Hayes Jacobs 1997, 5). Software packages such as Lotus notes make such an overview and true networking even more practical and manageable.

Mapping curriculum restores the big picture to a teacher, to a teacher team, or even to a whole district. The big picture is desperately needed in an environment that often focuses on minute details. Mapping curricula can reveal where duplications are occurring in how curriculum is actually taught in the classroom. In this way, it can be a tool to save time by avoiding unnecessary teaching of the same material in different courses or in different grades. While it is best for whole districts to help integrate curriculum by using curriculum mapping, even a single school, a single team, or an individual teacher could make use of this tool (Hayes Jacobs 1997). Curriculum mapping can help give the teacher a sense of control over the content, which is particularly critical when block scheduling is first introduced. Curriculum mapping can be a useful tool to aid the teacher in the transition to the new time organization that block scheduling represents. Finally, curriculum mapping can reveal ways that curriculum can be integrated, thus aiding in the process of making those connections for both teacher and student that can improve the long-term retention of curricular material.

Curriculum Integration

Some ten different models for integrating the curriculum have been identified: fragmented, connected, nested, sequenced, shared, webbed, threaded, integrated, immersed, and networked. Many of these models can be implemented with only two teachers. Obviously, more powerful connections can be made when more than two teachers work together in the process of integration. Figure 3.5 "Toward an Integrated Curriculum" provides definition for these types and examples.

Connections not only make better use of time but foster the kind of learning that sticks with students and enables them to see and make real-life applications. To venture into ways to integrate the curriculum is to question the way in which curricula is organized. "We continue to add things, but we seldomly take things out. How can we possibly teach everything when information today doubles every year and a half? One answer is restructuring schools from the inside out by reviewing the curriculum and setting priorities" (Fogarty and Stoehr 1995, 21).

Brain-Compatible Curriculum

Once the curricular content is identified it must be articulated in terms of brain-compatibility. No matter what group identified the content, Susan Kovalik (1997) asserts that it is a fundamental responsibility of the district to articulate the curriculum in terms of brain-compatibility. Brain-compatible curriculum is constructed and expressed in terms of concepts. Once identified at the local level, appropriate concepts must have at their core student success in life instead of student success in later schooling. She further suggests that curriculum is defined as brain-compatible if it...

- is conceptual versus "factoid" based
- has flexibility with direction
- includes the main idea (standard)
- has a rationale for inclusion, including the desired end result
- contains clearly defined concepts, making it clear to the practitioner what is meant and not meant
- includes expected student performance levels (criteria)

Active Instructional Material

A dynamic classroom does not use just one or two types of instructional materials. Instead, it makes use of a variety of instructional materials at one time or another. Luckily, the block class schedule allows time for students to use multiple sources, one of which is the computer. (See Appendix for electronic resources that enhance student learning via the Internet.) Traditional, static educational approaches rely heavily upon students gathering information from printed material and textbooks. Such sources have a clearly delineated beginning, middle, and end, which reinforces a linear way of thinking that may help students be successsful in school. For success in real life however, persons must process information and ideas from several sources. Electronic media offers the advantage of delivering information in a way that is more lifelike and allows students to construct a structure for the informa-

Toward an Integrated Curriculum

Ten Views for Integrating the Curricula: How Do You See It?

1

Fragmented
Periscope—one direction; one sighting; narrow focus on single discipline

Description
The traditional model of separate and distinct disciplines, which fragments the subject areas.

Example
Teacher applies this view in Math, Science, Social Studies, Language Arts OR Sciences, Humanities, Fine and Practical Arts.

2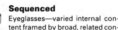

Connected
Opera glass—details of one discipline; focus on subtleties and interconnections

Description
Within each subject area, course content is connected topic to topic, concept to concept, one year's work to the next, and relates idea(s) explicitly.

Example
Teacher relates the concept of fractions to decimals, which in turn relates to money, grades, etc.

3

Nested
3-D glasses—multiple dimensions to one scene, topic, or unit

Description
Within each subject area, the teacher targets multiple skills: a social skill, a thinking skill, and a content-specific skill.

Example
Teacher designs the unit on photosynthesis to simultaneously target consensus seeking (social skill), sequencing (thinking skill), and plant life cycle (science content).

4

Sequenced
Eyeglasses—varied internal content framed by broad, related concepts

Description
Topics or units of study are rearranged and sequenced to coincide with one another. Similar ideas are taught in concert while remaining separate subjects.

Example
English teacher presents an historical novel depicting a particular period while the History teacher teaches that same historical period.

5

Shared
Binoculars—two disciplines that share overlapping concepts and skills

Description
Shared planning and teaching take place in two disciplines in which overlapping concepts or ideas emerge as organizing elements.

Example
Science and Math teachers use data collection, charting, and graphing as shared concepts that can be team-taught.

6

Webbed
Telescope—broad view of an entire constellation as one theme, webbed to the various elements

Description
A fertile theme is webbed to curriculum contents and disciplines; subjects use the theme to sift out appropriate concepts, topics, and ideas.

Example
Teacher presents a simple topical theme, such as the circus, and webs it to the subject areas. A conceptual theme, such as conflict, can be webbed for more depth in the theme approach.

7

Threaded
Magnifying glass—big ideas that magnify all content through a metacurricular approach

Description
The metacurricular approach threads thinking skills, social skills, multiple intelligences, technology, and study skills through the various disciplines.

Example
Teaching staff targets prediction in Reading, Math, and Science lab experiments while Social Studies teacher targets forecasting current events, and thus threads the skill (prediction) across disciplines. ♪

8

Integrated
Kaleidoscope—new patterns and designs that use the basic elements of each discipline

Description
This interdisciplinary approach matches subjects for overlaps in topics and concepts with some team teaching in an authentic integrated model.

Example
In Math, Science, Social Studies, Fine Arts, Language Arts, and Practical Arts, teachers look for patterning models and approach content through these patterns.

9

Immersed
Microscope—intensely personal view that allows microscopic explanation as all content is filtered through lens of interest and expertise

Description
The disciplines become part of the learner's lens of expertise; the learner filters all content through this lens and becomes immersed in his or her own experience.

Example
Student or doctoral candidate has an area of expert interest and sees all learning through that lens.

10

Networked
Prism—a view that creates multiple dimensions and directions of focus

Description
Learner filters all learning through the expert's eye and makes internal connections that lead to external networks of experts in related fields.

Example
Architect, while adapting the CAD/CAM technology for design, networks with technical programmers and expands her knowledge base, just as she had traditionally done with interior designers.

© Robin Fogarty, 1991

Figure 3.5

Adapted from *The Mindful School: How to Integrate the Curricula* by Robin Fogarty. ©1991 SkyLight Training and Publishing, Inc. Reprinted with permission of SkyLight Professional Development, Arlington Heights, IL.

tion that has personal meaning and that may not always be linear. Resources that allow students to bring their own experiences to bear on information, to discover new understandings, and to construct personal meaning are patently brain-compatible. In addition, electronic resources allow learning to be customized for the learner, which supports brain-comaptible learner-centered education (Tapscott 1999).

Sample Lesson Plan #3 illustrates a way that teachers can move beyond the textbook and the blackboard to illustrate a concept. In addition, it shows how the theme of circles is a magnet for content coverage. As presented here, *Circles That Cycle* is a lesson for elementary students, but teachers at any level can readily create a lesson, or even a unit, on circles (see Figure 3.3 "Circles Make the World Go 'Round" for ideas.) Teachers have a variety of options for developing student skills in measurement, understanding circular motion, and scientific investigation.

Sample Four-Phase Lesson Plan

Circles That Cycle

Level: Elementary

Curriculum Integration: Math, Science, and Physical Education

Multiple Intelligences

- ☑ Bodily/Kinesthetic
- ☑ Interpersonal
- ❑ Intrapersonal
- ☑ Logical/Mathematical

- ❑ Musical
- ❑ Naturalist
- ☑ Verbal/Linguistic
- ☑ Visual/Spatial

Content Standards

MATHEMATICS

Understands and applies basic and advanced properties of the concepts of measurement

Understands and applies basic and advanced properties of the concepts of geometry

PHYSICAL SCIENCES

Understands motion and the principles that explain it

Knows the relationship between the strength of a force and its effect on an object (e.g., the greater the force, the greater the change in motion; the more massive the object, the smaller the effect of a given force)

SCIENCE (NATURE)

Understands the nature of scientific inquiry

PHYSICAL EDUCATION

Uses a variety of basic and advanced movement forms

INQUIRE PHASE
15 MINUTES

Inquire Activity Option A

Objective: Students physically uncover the concepts related to the parts of a circle and the distance across versus the distance around it.

ATTEND

The teacher asks . . .

- What makes a circle a circle?
- What's the difference between a circle, an oval, and an oblong?
- How can we set up our chairs in a circle? Please do it.

EXPERIENCE: "ANYBODY WHO"

The teacher . . .

- Arranges chairs in a large circle and instructs students to sit in a chair (no empty chairs should be left in the circle)
- Stands in the center of the circle to begin (the only person without a chair).
- Teaches the phrase: Anybody Who _____.
  Fill in the blank with a characteristic. Potential characteristics can include:
  Behavior: sleeps on his or her stomach, likes to dance, reads comics, and eats ice cream
  Clothing: wears a watch, has on jewelry, wears socks
- Tells students to state a characteristic that applies to some or all of them. If the characteristic fits them, they must quickly move to another chair (at least two chairs away) as you (the teacher) also move to an unoccupied chair.
- Explains that since there is one more person than chairs, one student will be left standing. This person then repeats "Anybody Who" and names another characteristic.

REFLECT

The teacher asks . . .

- How many of you ran to a chair following the circumference of our circled chairs? The diameter? The radius?
- What was the quickest way to get to an empty chair?
- What would happen to the game if we made the circle smaller? Bigger?

Inquire Activity Option B

Objective: Students physically demonstrate the meaning of words related to the measurement of a circle.

ATTEND

While students continue to sit in the circled chairs, the teacher . . .

- Draws a circle on the board or chart paper, assigns students to pairs, and asks them to draw and label as many parts of a circle as they can on a piece of chart paper.
- Directs student pairs to share their labeled circles with other pairs.
- Refers to the circle on the board, asks the groups to indicate the parts of a circle they identified, and writes them on the circle.
- Fills in any parts of the circle the students don't provide, which may include: circumference, radius, diameter, degrees (360, 180, 90), radian, and pi depending on class readiness and level.
- Passes out a piece of paper to each student with five circle drawn on it.
- Completes an observation log while the students perform (see Figure 3.7).

Students . . .

- "Act out" the following by moving around or through the circle of chairs one by one:
  – circumference
  – degree
  – diameter
  – radian
  – radius
- Illustrate the above five words by drawing and labeling each circle on the sheet the teacher passed out.

Observation Log

Focus Components	Observation
Parts of a circle	*Audrey, Jose, and Kim remained unsure of how to act out the radius. Several other students were unclear regarding the concept of degrees of a circle.* *Design an experience that would mediate these difficulties, decide what phase such an experience would work into.*
Student interaction	*Jamal helped explain the concept of radian to Geoff and the rest of the class by stationing three students at points on the circle.* *Generally students' demonstrations at the end of the line were modeling earlier student representations, which helped the more reluctant and unsure students be confident of their demonstration and set the state for the later phases of the lesson.*
Reasoning	*Most of the students were able to exlain their movements and why they made them. Pam and Lewis were better able to illustrate the concepts on paper using fine motor skills than they were at using the gross motor skills of demonstrating with physical action.*

Figure 3.6

REFLECT

The teacher asks the following questions . . .

- Demonstrating which part of the circle took the most energy? Why?
- Demonstrating which part of the circle took the least energy? Why?
- We used footsteps to measure the length of the parts of a circle. What tool is most appropriately used to do that?

GATHER PHASE

35 MINUTES

Gather Activity

Objective: Students study a multi-speed bike and the gearshift components and label circle parts on the wheel, gearshift wheels, and chain. Students demonstrate how the size of a "circle" effects effort and speed. Students previously volunteered to bring multi-speed bikes with gearshifting capabilities to class. One bike is needed for every four students.

ATTEND

The teacher . . .

- Asks one student to volunteer to bring a bike to the front of the room.
- Provides students with rulers or tape measure, piece of string, masking tape, chalk, and a large protractor.
- Can model how to use the simple tools or allow students to problem-solve how to use the implements.

Students . . .

- Guided by the teacher, label the parts of a circle on one of the bicycle wheels.
- Measure changes in distance the bike travels as students shift front and back gears.
- Examine their multi-speed bikes in their small groups and observe what happens to the pedal speed, wheel distance, and pedal difficulty during various gear shifting positions.
- Take the bicycles outside to ride them as part of their data gathering.
- Record their observations (see Figure 3.7).
- Work with other groups after completing their observation logs to share and compare their observations.

Student Observation Log

Group Members:		Date:	
Gear Shifting	**Pedal Speed** faster/slower	**Wheel Distance** more/less	**Pedaling Difficulty** easier/harder
Front chain on largest sprocket and back chain on largest sprocket			
Front chain on largest sprocket and back chain on smallest sprocket			
Front chain on middle sprocket and back chain on largest sprocket			
Front chain on middle sprocket and back chain on smallest sprocket			
Front chain on smallest sprocket and back chain on largest sprocket			
Front chain on smallest sprocket and back chain on smallest sprocket			
Comments:			

Figure 3.7

The teacher . . .

- Leads a class discussion of the students' bicycle observations, clarifying any misunderstandings or misperceptions.

EXPERIENCE

Students, while still in their small groups . . .

- Demonstrate the impact circle size has on effort and speed. For example: form a crack-the-whip-line to show how slowly the inside person rotates compared to the person who is walking very quickly on the outside.
- Spin with arms extended out compared to spinning with arms folded.
- Jump rope with a large rope compared to a small rope.

REFLECT

Teacher asks . . .

- What have you learned about circles you never knew before?
- What is the greatest thing you learned about how bikes work?
- What can you teach your friends about bikes you think they don't understand?
- How can you use your understanding of circles when you play with friends?

PROCESS PHASE
20 MINUTES

Process Activity

Objective: Students prepare a quiz game on circles.

Students . . .

- As a class, brainstorm four to six categories for a *Jeopardy*-style game, "What's the Question?"

ATTEND

The teacher . . .

- Assigns one student group to each category to prepare at least five answers and their questions for each category
- Monitors groups and facilitates answer and question preparation.

Students play the game by the following rules:

- One group chooses a category.
- Teacher reads the answer.
- Each of the groups has fifteen seconds to write their response to the answer.
- When time is called, students hold up their questions.
- Each group with a correct question gets the points.

REFLECT

The teacher asks the following questions . . .

- What did you like most about preparing and playing the game, "What's the Question?"
- How did preparing the answers and questions help clarify the information?
- What can you do to make sure you "know that you know" all that we learned today?
- If you were to tell your family one thing you learned from today's lesson, what would that be? Tell your partner.

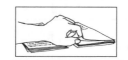

APPLY PHASE
20 MINUTES

Apply Activity Option A

Objective: Students participate in a mini field trip to "hunt" for circles on the school grounds.

ATTEND

The teacher . . .

- Facilitates grouping students into small groups of two or three students to participate in a treasure hunt for circles.
- Asks students to think of all the items that have circular shapes either in the school building or out on the school grounds. Calls on three or four students to share their ideas.

EXPERIENCE: "CIRCLE SCAVENGER HUNT"

Students . . .

- Find as many circles as they can and record the ways circles are used on an observation log (see Figure 3.8 "Circle Scavenger Hunt Log").
- Return to class to share the examples they found.

Circle Scavenger Hunt Log

Names:				Date:	

For each circle you find, record the following:
1. Describe the circle.
2. Identify where you observed it.
3. Note the parts of the circle that are evident.
4. Explain the function or purpose of the particular circle.
5. List examples of other circles you previously observed elsewhere.

	Describe	Where Observed	Circle Parts	Purpose or Function	Other Examples
Circle #1					
Circle # 2					
Circle # 3					
Circle # 4					
Circle # 5					
Circle # 6					

Figure 3.8

REFLECT

The teacher asks the following questions . . .

- What do you see in circles now that you didn't see before? Tell a neighbor.
- What's one thing you understand now that didn't make sense to you earlier?
- What will you do differently now that you understand circles better?

Apply Activity Option B

Objective: Students work together to create a song or design a machine using "circle" concepts.

ATTEND

Teacher . . .

- Facilitates grouping students into small groups of two or three students to participate in creating a song or designing a machine to reflect their understanding of circles.

EXPERIENCE: "RAP UP"

Students either . . .

- Make up words about circles that fit a familiar "round" and sing it. (This is more appropriate for younger elementary level students) or
- In small groups, create a machine that uses circles. (This is more appropriate for upper level elementary students.)

REFLECT

Students complete a self-assessment of their presentation. See Figure 3.9 "Student Self-Assessment."

Student Self-Assessment

1. Did my song include a mention of each of the circle's five parts we studied today?

YES	NO	MAYBE

2. Did I sing out clearly so the whole class could easily understand what I was saying?

YES	NO	MAYBE

3. Did I work well and cooperatively with the members of my group?

YES	NO	MAYBE

4. Did I make an important contribution to my group's successful performance?

YES	NO	MAYBE

5. Did creating and performing our song help me to remember the parts of a circle?

YES	NO	MAYBE

6. Overall how would you rate your contrubution to the performance?

Excellent	Very Good	Good	Okay	Could Have Done Better

7. Explain the rating you gave yourself.

Figure 3.9

CHAPTER 4

INSTRUCTION
THE ART AND SCIENCE OF TEACHING IN THE BLOCK

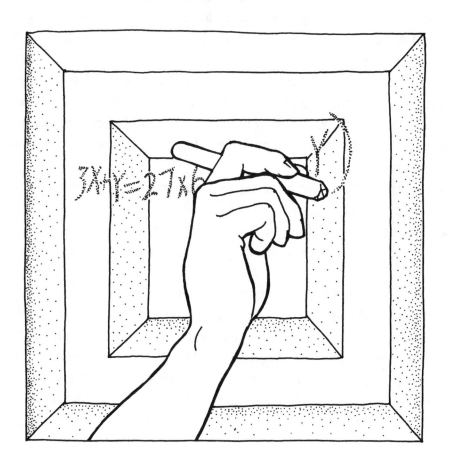

Block scheduling without fundamental changes in instruction is merely longer blocks of the same old stuff. If improved learning is the goal, instructional practices will have to change in order to best take advantage of the opportunity of longer blocks of time.

—Linda Wyatt 1996, 18

Opportunity for Growth and Change

Many teachers accustomed to a forty-five or fifty minute class period are apprehensive about the prospect of filling up twice that amount of time (or more) in an extended time block. Underlying their concern is the question of how to keep students interested and motivated for such an extended period. Both concerns find their answers in brain-compatible pedagogy.

The teacher in the block has the opportunity to orchestrate the curriculum and instruction into events, projects, environments, and graphics that can assist student learning. Such an opportunity calls for sophisticated pedagogy that goes beyond imparting data through lecturing or assigned readings. Instead, it demands strategies that enable information and concepts to be learned through challenges, questions, problems, and situations that encourage students to become interested, research the relevant and appropriate information, process it, and apply it—in other words, learning that is brain compatible. Such a dynamic, interconnected, surprise-filled, challenging environment is more feasible in extended class formats than in shorter bell schedule periods.

Students' brains are far more capable than traditional formats have allowed for; therefore, teachers need to

- Design lessons rich in sensory experiences
- Use the whole body in learning with movement and hands-on experience
- Involve a wide range of emotions and intelligences.

Not only do the above strategies make good use of the additional time, but they also make it much easier to use brain-compatible teaching principles (Fitzgerald 1996). Further, in traditional scheduling, after offering content material teachers would need to wait until the following day for processing and application activities, often needing to review the content-heavy material previously presented before moving on to the higher-order activities.

Energizing Educational Principles

Although there may be others, four educational principles (pulsed learning, teaching to long-term memory, beginning-end-middle principle, and varying instructional strategies) help to energize and enhance a teacher's pedagogical

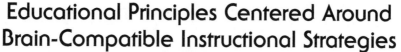

Educational Principles Centered Around Brain-Compatible Instructional Strategies

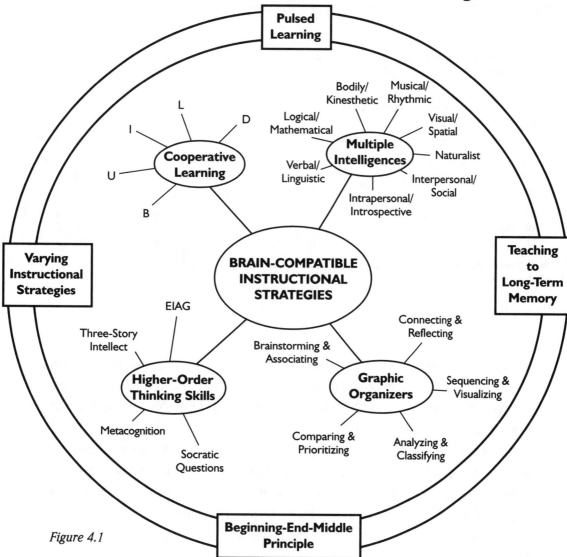

Figure 4.1

repertoire. (See Figure 4.1 "Educational Principles Centered Around Brain-Compatible Instructional Strategies" for a representation of this dynamic.)

Pulsed Learning

Ron Fitzgerald (1996) suggests the concept of *pulsed learning,* which simply stated is that an activity requiring a high degree of concentration needs to be followed by an activity that is more relaxed and allows for the processing of

Pulsed Learning

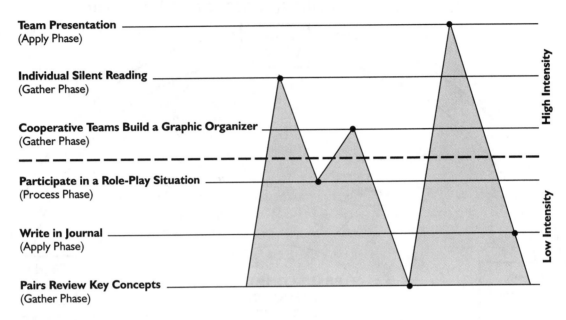

Team Presentation
(Apply Phase)

Individual Silent Reading
(Gather Phase)

Cooperative Teams Build a Graphic Organizer
(Gather Phase)

Participate in a Role-Play Situation
(Process Phase)

Write in Journal
(Apply Phase)

Pairs Review Key Concepts
(Gather Phase)

High Intensity

Low Intensity

Figure 4.2

material absorbed in the high-concentration activity. A class period of lecture, video, and a quiz is composed of all high-concentration activities. Figure 4.2 depicts the relative intensity of some activities and how that can help teachers plot a course for learning.

In order to get a handle on high-concentration versus low-concentration activities, teachers can make a list of the kinds of activities and strategies that require a great deal of focus and intense attention (high concentration) and a separate list of the kinds of activities and strategies that are more relaxed and require less active attention (low concentration). Creating such lists is a great activity for a teacher team to engage in.

Teaching to Long-Term Memory

As discussed in chapter 1, memorization occurs in a part of the brain with limited holding capacity. Unless the information is connected to previously learned information, unless the information is put into some meaningful framework, or unless the information is applied to daily life in some way, then the information stays in short-term memory and gets crowded out with the next deluge of data (Sylwester 1995). Such a simple concept, however, has obvious consequences for how curriculum is taught. This is not to suggest that discrete data and information are unimportant. Rather, it is possible to convey important data and information with concepts, frameworks, and connections in such a way that the brain can retain the information much longer than through rote memorization processes. Brain-compatible instructional methods that best foster long-term memory are most effectively employed in an extended time format.

Most every discipline has core facts and crucial pieces of information that are essential for students to learn. It is part of the teacher's job to know what they are. Reading current material, attending content area classes, and maintaining a dialogue with departmental and grade-level colleagues all help teachers remain abreast of the detailed information attendant to the content area for which they are responsible. The next step is to discern what activity or experience will enable that material to be conveyed in a way that is meaningful and makes sense.

In other words, it is not enough to know what facts are important for the students to grasp. What is needed is for teachers to help content material permeate long-term memory, where it will be readily available for use in some later real-life situation or even in some later test. Figure 4.3 "Brain-Compatible Methods of Content Presentation" shows some actual course content and some alternative (brain-compatible) settings in which to deliver that course content.

Brain-Compatible Methods of Content Presentation

Course Content	Alternative Settings
Vocabulary	Real-life Stories by Students
Historical Dates	Timelines or Museum Trips
Factual Data	Charts or Matrices
Historical Events	Role Playing
General Concepts	Debates or Graphic Organizers
Scientific Concepts	Lab Experiments or Cyber Field Trips to Relevant Web Sites

Figure 4.3

The Beginning-End-Middle (BEM) Principle

Fitzgerald (1996) notes that students are most attentive at the beginning and the end of any one learning strategy and least attentive in the middle. He articulated this as the Beginning-End-Middle (BEM) Principle. If a ninety-minute lesson has basically just one learning approach, there will be a rather large "middle" section during which attention dramatically falls off. Therefore, by utilizing more learning strategies or activities, one necessarily decreases the number of less attentive "middles" and increases the number of more attentive "beginnings" and "ends." The BEM principle aligns directly with the Four-Phase Lesson Design promoted throughout this book, which assumes that any one lesson will have a variety of activities interspersed throughout the ninety minutes. If an entire class period is devoted to one activity, energy will inevitably wane (this is especially true of a class period in excess of 100 minutes.) The Four-Phase lesson design builds upon this idea to propose that the activities within the lesson (as well as the lessons within the unit) should be organized to culminate in students working with the material in some authentic and meaningful way. (See chapter 6 for an extensive discussion of constructing brain-compatible lessons for the extended time block.)

There are several concerns that the teacher in extended time formats needs to keep in mind. When it is suggested that several strategies are used to increase the beginnings and ends, the activities still need to be meaningful and connected to the content—not simply activities for activities' sake. A variety of strategies that illuminate the desired curriculum objectives, however, can actually make the content come alive in ways not experienced by students before. Furthermore, diverse strategies can enable the teacher to reach a broader base of students than perhaps have previously been touched.

Varying Instructional Strategies

What is *done* with the time is more important than the *length* of time itself. The key to increasing student attention is expanding the variety of instructional strategies and approaches (Rettig and Canady 1996). Learning and attention are enhanced when there are shifts from one approach to another within the ninety minute period, or within the fifty minute period for that matter. Blending cooperative learning strategies, multiple intelligence theory, higher-order thinking tasks, and information managing tools such as graphic organizers call forth the very attentiveness and desire to learn from students that teachers want to capture.

Brain-Compatible Instructional Strategies

In brain-compatible instruction, students become fully involved in their learning. The teacher guides or leads students to the sources of knowledge. Consequently, students and teachers are traveling companions on the journey of learning. In this way, students discover how to solve real-life problems, how to find the answers when the answers are not immediately available, and how to adapt when yesterday's answers no longer fit today's problems. Using brain-compatible learning strategies can help aid in the advance of information from the short-term working memory system to the long-term memory system, promoting learning for life and not just for a test.

Cooperative Learning Approaches

It is well stated by Robert Sylwester that the central reason for the success of cooperative group activities when used well is that "[s]uch activities . . . place students at the center of the educative process, and thus stimulate learning" (Sylwester 1995, 132). As a consequence, motivation runs high; learning runs deep; and time passes quickly. Ultimately, the skills students gain from working in a cooperative fashion are the very same skills that have become inextricably woven into a great number of the jobs and careers students are in training for today (Fitzgerald 1996). Cooperative skills are becoming as important in the world of work as knowledge and technological skills.

David Johnson, Roger Johnson, and E. J. Holubec (1988) offer five elements of fruitful cooperative learning: positive interdependence, individual accountability, group processing, face-to-face interaction, and collaborative skills. James Bellanca and Robin Fogarty (1991) use the acronym BUILD as the basis of creating cooperative learning lessons:

Bring in higher-order thinking
Unite the teams and the class
Insure individual learning and accountability
Look over, step back, and discuss
Develop social skills

Figure 4.4 "B.U.I.L.D. Cooperative Learning Fundamentals" provides an overview of the cooperative learning process.

BRING IN HIGHER-ORDER THINKING

Each cooperative learning approach needs to embody some higher-order thinking skill or process. A significant higher-order thinking challenge is one way to make the cooperative experience a richer, more profound one than studying alone. (See the Higher-Order Thinking Skills section of this chapter for elaboration of that concept.)

UNIFY THE TEAMS AND THE CLASS

The use of heterogeneous groups actually helps individuals discover that all the gifts of their fellow members are needed to accomplish the assigned work. Cooperative learning groups

- Have an assigned role for each person
- Learn explicit social skills
- Are given a challenging task demanding the participation of all
- Are given tasks that weave in higher-order thinking
- Are usually heterogeneous in makeup
- Frequently reflect and process how they are learning and how they are working together as a team.

INSURE INDIVIDUAL LEARNING AND ACCOUNTABILITY

It is the teacher's task to formulate activities in which individual learning and accountability can be guaranteed. Getting an accurate picture of the individual learning removes one common criticism of cooperative learning structures often voiced by parents and students—that one person is too often burdened with all of the work.

LOOK OVER, STEP BACK, AND DISCUSS

An integral part of a lesson is the opportunity to step back and talk about what has just occurred. The key to this is questions that the teacher prepares ahead of time. These questions may focus on the content of the lesson, the methods used in the lesson, or the experience of working as a group. Some students may only make sense of the lesson at this point. The extended class

B.U.I.L.D. Cooperative Learning Fundamentals

Key Questions	B	U	I	L	D
What is the Acronym?					
What Do the Letters Stand For?	Bring in Higher Order Thinking	Unify the Teams and the Class	Insure Individual Learning and Accountability	Look Over, Step Back, and Discuss	Develop Social Skills
What Is Its Function?	To utilize the gifts of the collaborative setting to intensify the cognitive	To create bonding and connections among students in the class and on a team	To make sure that rigorous individual learning is taking place	To reflect on the material learned and the experience of learning To help the learning and the experience really belong to the learner	To deepen students' abilities to interact so that the learning can be deeper and richer among the team and among the class
What Are Some Ways to Do This In the Classroom?	Teaching Thinking Skills Directly Graphic Organizers Fat & Skinny Questions	Assigned Roles One Set of Materials Call for One Product From the Team Team Name, Symbol, Slogan	Random Oral Quizzes Tests Conferences Assigned Section within a Team Project	Reflection Questions P.M.I. Chart Team Self-Assessing Checklists	Teaching social skills directly Team roles of encourager or observer "That's a good idea because . . ."

Figure 4.4 Adapted from *Blueprints for Thinking in the Cooperative Classroom* by James Bellanca and Robin Fogarty. © 1991 IRI/SkyLight Training and Publishing, Inc. Reprinted with permission of SkyLight Professional Development, Arlington Heights, IL.

format permits the time to do this job adequately. Even if there are only three or four minutes to do this kind of processing, it is crucial to student learning.

DEVELOP SOCIAL SKILLS

The teacher is called on to teach social skills directly, to provide actual practice time to make the skills automatic and natural, and finally to monitor the ongoing utilization of these skills. It is important to teach social skills in nearly the same way a content discipline is taught throughout the semester. In other words, the teacher cannot assume the students are experienced in the use of social skills on the first day of class. Likewise, the teacher can't teach all of the necessary skills at once. Deciding which skills are most important and focusing on those and phasing others in later is part of the role of the teacher.

Implications for the Extended Time Format

Cooperative learning approaches are crucial for the extended class format because they
- Provide a shift in the intensity of learning activities
- Offer an opportunity for interaction that students appreciate
- Encourage higher-order thinking as content material is worked on and used
- Can help the teacher cover large amounts of material by dividing it among several groups to study and then present to the larger group.

MULTIPLE INTELLIGENCES

Multiple intelligence (MI) theory, as pioneered by Howard Gardner (1983), emphasizes the importance of personal meaning-making and problem solving. In the traditional classroom, either out of habit or convention, most of the activities are based on lecture and computation, which play to only two (verbal/linguistic and logical/mathematical) of the eight intelligences. Conversely, as has been suggested here, brain-compatible instructional strategies such as cooperative learning help develop interpersonal skills (interpersonal intelligence) and at the same time include as many of the other intelligences as possible. (See Figure 4.5 for a list of the types of activities that exercise each intelligence.) Such activities promote cognitive development through intrinsic motivation, which leads to student desire for lifelong learning and inquiry. Perhaps MI theory benefits education the most in that it necessitates the expansion of teaching repertoire, which in turn has positive implications for teaching in the block.

Higher-Order Thinking Skills

Benjamin S. Bloom's *Taxonomy* (1956) proposes a hierarchy of thinking processes that move from the most basic, *knowledge*, through *comprehension, application, analysis*, and *synthesis*, culminating in *evaluation*. The more advanced and intricate thinking processes are therefore referred to as *higher-order thinking skills*. Teachers have been challenged for years to ask students to think in a variety of ways. The highly specialized and technology-driven world in which educators and students alike live demands critical thinking and reasoning as never before. The following approaches can be used to elicit higher-order thinking from students.

The Socratic Method

Socrates applied reasoning to arrive at truth by asking questions. He didn't lecture or provide answers. He used inductive reasoning instead of relying on traditional thinking ("Everybody thinks this way" or "We've always done it like that") or prescribed doctrine ("We think only what we've been told to think" or "I read it somewhere so it must be true").

Socratic irony was his search for truth by assuming he knew nothing about the topic and that he must question everything to arrive finally at truth.

Socrates is famous for creating conceptual conflicts with his questioning techniques. Persons engaged in dialogue with Socrates would then have to revisit what they thought they knew and rethink their position. Teachers can use a similar technique when asking students to actively process new information or learning activities.

By asking questions instead of providing information or lectures, teachers are helping students to think, to discover truth, and to make sense of the topic of the lesson. Socrates was so successful in his approach to learning and discovery that his technique has survived for more than two thousand years.

Gardner's Eight Intelligences

Visual/Spatial

Images, graphics, drawings, sketches, maps, charts, doodles, pictures, spatial orientation, puzzles, designs, looks, appeal, mind's eye, imagination, visualization, dreams, nightmares, films, and videos.

Logical/Mathematical

Reasoning, deductive and inductive logic, facts, data, information, spreadsheets, databases, sequencing, ranking, organizing, analyzing, proofs, conclusions, judging, evaluations, and assessments.

Verbal/Linguistic

Words, wordsmiths, speaking, writing, listening, reading, papers, essays, poems, plays, narratives, lyrics, spelling, grammar, foreign languages, memos, bulletins, newsletters, newspapers, E-mail, FAXes, speeches, talks, dialogues, and debates.

Musical/Rhythmic

Music, rhythm, beat, melody, tunes, allegro, pacing, timbre, tenor, soprano, opera, baritone, symphony, choir, chorus, madrigals, rap, rock, rhythm and blues, jazz, classical, folk, ads and jingles.

Bodily/Kinesthetic

Art, activity, action, experiental, hands-on, experiments, try, do, perform, play, drama, sports, throw, toss, catch, jump, twist, twirl, assemble, disassemble, form, re-form, manipulate, touch, feel, immerse, and participate.

Interpersonal/Social

Interact, communicate, converse, share, understand, empathize, sympathize, reach out, care, talk whisper, laugh, cry, shudder, socialize, meet, greet, lead, follow, gangs, clubs, charisma, crowds, gatherings, and twosomes.

Intrapersonal/Introspective

Self, solitude, meditate, think, create, brood, reflect, envision, journal, self-assess, set goals, plot, plan, dream, write, fiction, nonfiction, poetry, affirmations, lyrics, songs, screenplays, commentaries, introspection, and inspection.

Naturalist

Nature, natural, environment, listen, watch, observe, classify, categorize, discern patterns, appreciate, hike, climb, fish, hunt, snorkle, dive, photograph, trees, leaves, animals, living things, flora, fauna, ecosystem, sky, grass, mountains, lakes, and rivers.

Figure 4.5

Adapted from *Problem-Based Learning and Other Curriculum Models for the Multiple Intelligences Classroom* by Robin Fogarty. ©1997 by SkyLight Training and Publishing Inc. Reprinted with permission of SkyLight Professional Development, Arlington Heights, IL.

Metacognition

Metacognition is the key to helping students make sense of the information, thoughts, and feelings they encounter during each learning experience of the unit. As teachers guide students through processing and reflecting on each activity, they help students think about their random, divergent, and disconnected thoughts and transition those thoughts to understand not only what they experienced but what meaning they can derive from the experience.

An important aspect of metacognition is the kind of learning experiences teachers select for their students. Without stimulating, complex, and challenging experiences, metacognitive reflections would be nothing more than students recalling information or the rote memorization of facts and details. Caine and Caine (1997) challenge teachers to design experiences that will facilitate the "ah-ha" moment as well as provide opportunities for frequent meta-questioning throughout the experience.

Students can also learn to ask themselves metacognitive questions as they engage in various learning activities. In this way they become aware of their own learning and thinking processes.

The Three-Story Intellect Model

James Bellanca and Robin Fogarty (1991) have constructed the concept of the three-story intellect based on a quote by Oliver Wendell Holmes. The three stories (floors in a building) refer to levels of understanding and the sequence of the steps in achieving the highest level that would allow one to apply all that has been gathered and processed. The four-phase lesson design examples throughout this book are built upon the three-story intellect but add the *inquire* phase before Bellanca and Fogarty's "first story" of gathering. (See Figure 4.6 "The Three-Story Intellect.")

Experience/Identify/Apply/Generalize

The acronym EIAG is an active processing model developed by H. Stephen Glenn (Glenn and Nelson 1988). This circular model shows that the thinking process is continuous and reflective and that the questions remain linked to the learning activity.

E (experience) refers to questions that ask students to reflect on the experience they have had. Even though teachers design learning activities to be consistent for each student—the same lab experiment, same chapter to study, same novel to read, same homework assignments—the reaction of each student to the learning activity may vary widely. What one student observes, attends to, feels, and thinks about might be something completely different from other students because of the difference in their previous experiences, skill levels, and understanding. Each learning activity, therefore, can be quite different for each student. Questions asking students to reflect on what their experiences were provide all students with diverse insights into what others encountered. They can appreciate diverse perspectives as a result of their shared differences.

Examples of **E** questions:
- What just happened?
- What was your experience in the class?
- What did you observe during the activity?
- What was the sequence of events?

I (identify) questions direct students to contemplate four different thinking tasks. This category of questions asks students to describe what their thoughts were, what subsequent feelings, attitudes, or moods they experienced, what changes in their behaviors occurred, and what new discoveries, insights, or perceptions resulted from the experience.

Examples of **I** questions:
- What were you thinking about during the activity?
- How did you feel about the successes and failures of the experience?
- What did you do differently from what you thought you were going to do?
- What new insights did you gain from the activity?
- What changes in perception occurred as a result of the experience?

A (analyze) questions require the students to examine the "whys" of their thoughts, feelings, behaviors, and understandings. Why do they feel the way they do? Why do they think what they are thinking? Why did they act the way they did? Where did their insights come from? What connections did they make?

Examples of **A** questions:
- What influenced your thoughts during the activity?
- How did your thoughts change your feelings during the experience?

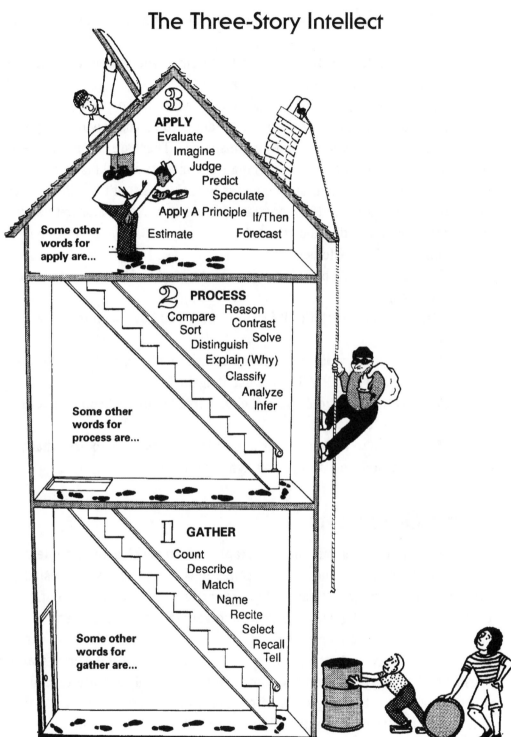

The Three-Story Intellect

Figure 4.6

From *Patterns for Thinking, Patterns for Transfer* by Robin Fogarty and James Bellanca. ©1993 by IRI/SkyLight Publishing, Inc. Reprinted with permission of SkyLight Professional Development, Arlington Heights, IL.

- Which thoughts and feelings had the greatest impact on your behaviors?
- What connections did you make that helped you understand the concepts and make sense of the activity?
- How did your perceptions change as a result of the experience?

G (generalize) questions encourage students to consider ways to apply the skills and information to other circumstances. These questions can help students make the transfer from learning the concepts and skills in the classroom to applying these skills and concepts in real-life situations. These questions provide relevancy and demonstrate various contexts of alternative ways to use the classroom skills and concepts.

Examples of **G** questions:

- Where might you be able to apply what you have learned outside this classroom?
- Describe some real-life situations where you have seen these skills used.
- What response would you give to someone who asks, "Why do I have to learn this stuff? Will I ever use it again?"
- What connections did you make with this lesson and some of your past experiences?
- If you were to write a prescription of when and how to use what you have learned from this lesson, what would it be?

Graphic Organizers

As discussed in the previous chapter, graphic organizers are tools students can use to aid in such thought and organizational processes as synthesizing information, constructing relationships, identifying associations, making connections, organizing data, analyzing and generating ideas, and exploring shared attributes of concepts. Students can further use graphic organizers to order, sort, classify, and arrange their thinking. Implicit in the name "graphic organizers" is the visual component of this tool. Not only are students able to practice numerous thinking skills with graphic organizers, but they are also able to organize their thoughts and to capture their thinking visually.

Figure 4.7 "Graphic Organizers" makes the connection between the use of graphic orgainizers and the higher-order thinking skills they exercise. In addition, the figure provides a visual illustration of each of the seventeen types discussed below.

Concept Web

The inner circle represents the major concept or topic, key theme, or main idea to explore. The lines that extend away from the circle and end in smaller circles are subtopics or minor themes of the main idea. Lines and bubbles that emanate from the subtopic circles are sub-subtopic points. Students can use this graphic organizers to explore shared attributes of a topic or concept and to construct the relationship of subtopics, sub-subtopics, etc., with the topic. For example, in a science class, students explore the details of invertebrates (topic), locomotion (subtopic), and various types of locomotion (sub-subtopic).

Mind Map

This is similar to a concept web and sunshine wheel in structure. The primary difference is that instead of words captured in circles or bubbles, ideas are represented by pictures or visuals. Students can use this graphic organizer to illustrate ideas visually instead of using words. For example, in an algebra class, students can explore uses of quadratic equations through pictures that represent appropriate applications. In a foreign language class it could be used to represent various definitions and appropriate use of specific words or phrases.

Sunshine Wheel

The circle is the topic, issue, cue, or suggestion and the lines extending out from the inner circle, like rays of sunshine, indicate insights and ideas generated as a result of thinking about the topic. Students can use this graphic organizer to generate ideas or brainstorm suggestions. For example, in an English class, students can brainstorm ideas for a short story they are to write as well as possible plot lines, characters, and setting among other things.

Venn Diagram

In its most frequent use, two overlapping circles are used to show the unique characteristics and shared characteristics of two topics. However, other

Graphic Organizers

Brainstorming and Associating	Comparing and Prioritizing	Analyzing and Classifying	Sequencing and Visualizing	Connecting and Reflecting
Concept Web	Venn Diagram	Fishbone	Bridging Snapshots	KWL
Mind Map	Analogy/Simile Chart ___ is like ___ Because 1. 2. 3. Visual Representation	Matrix	Looks-Sounds-Feels Looks | Sounds | Feels	KDL
Sunshine Wheel	T-Chart	Double T-Chart	Pie Chart	PMI P M I
	Ranking Ladder			Right Angle

Figure 4.7

shapes can be used. In the area where the shapes overlap, elements that are shared or held in common are identified. In the non-overlapping space, elements unique to each are listed. Students can use this graphic organizer to construct relationships and show differences. For example, in a biology class, sea lions and walrus can be compared/contrasted. In a music class, spirituals and country/ western music can be compared/contrasted. In Four-Phase Lesson Plan #2: *Can Prejudice Kill a Mockingbird?* students are asked to construct a Venn diagram comparing/contrasting characters in the novel *To Kill a Mockingbird*.

Analogy/Simile Chart

Unfamiliar concepts are compared to something that is familiar and known or understood.

Students can use analogies as a graphic organizer to visually represent the relationship between divergent or disparate entities, one of which is clearly understood, the other is not. The comparison assists the students' understanding of the difficult concept. For example, in a high school science class an analogy can be made for the function of an enzyme. An enzyme is like a (blank) because (blank).

T-Chart

Information is organized in two columns with headings such as (a) pre- and post-, (b) before and after, (c) pros and cons, (d) either/or, (e) better and worse, and (f) benefits and detriments. Students can use this graphic organizer to synthesize information and record it. For example, in a geography class, students can compare Poland's political and socioeconomic situation before and after the Solidarity movement. And in a psychology class they can identify the pros and cons of Freud's psychotherapy process.

Ranking Ladder

What is the rank order of the data? How is the information prioritized? What is most important and what is least important? Students can use this graphic organizer to prioritize, order, or rank data and information. For example, in a business class, students rank the following budget items in terms of most important to least important: research and development, personnel training, advertising, facility and building upkeep, and technology.

Fishbone

The head of the fishbone, or box, represents a problem to solve, an issue to address, or an event to plan. The bones along the body represent the causes of the problem and solutions for each cause, major components of an issue with accompanying details, or essential elements of an event and specifics of each. Students can use this graphic organizer to identify associations, solve problems, address issues, or analyze details. For example, in a sociology class, students can address the glass-ceiling problem in America and suggest ways to resolve the issue.

Matrix/Grid

Any number of intersecting horizontal and vertical lines are used to classify, compare, and categorize. Elements are listed on the left column and characteristics for comparison or analysis are used to label the subsequent columns of the grid. Students can use this graphic organizers to analyze details and classify data. The matrix can be helpful in making decisions, drawing conclusions, or making inferences. For example, in a language arts class, students can identify characters in a novel or play and evaluate each character for strengths, weaknesses, roles, contribution to the story, and relationship to other characters.

Double T-Chart

This is similar to a T-Chart in function, but instead of two columns there are three. Students can use this graphic organizer to synthesize information or data and arrange it into three categories. For example, in a physics class, students can list the effects of gravity on three things: mass and weight, fluid dynamics, and motion. And in a theatre class, students can reflect on the impact of a play they have performed by identifying, *what* they learned, *so what* did the play mean to them, *now what* will they do with the information. KWL, KDL, and Looks-Sounds-Feels are types of Double T-Charts.

Bridging Snapshots

Sequence charts, flowcharts, storyboards, or timetables are used to show succession of information in which students can make connections sequentially. For example, in a physiology class, students can sequence the steps an impulse follows from the brain to the motor unit to a muscle fiber to the return to homeostasis. In a technology class, students can design a storyboard of the sequence of camera shots they will take to create a public service advertisement.

Looks-Sounds-Feels

What does it *look* like (relative to its behaviors, physical characteristics, or visual qualities)? What does it *sound* like (its message or meaning, auditory or acoustic characteristics, or tonal qualities)? What does it *feel* like (its emotions, sensations or sensitivity, its tangible or material characteristics, or tactile qualities)? Students can use this graphic organizer to explore shared attributes. For example, in a biology class, what does a whale look like, sound like, feel like? And in a psychology class, what does a bipolar condition look like, sound like, feel like?

Pie Chart

The pie represents the whole, the big picture, or the entire set of data or information. The segments or slices of the pie represent parts, fractions, or percentages of the whole. Students can use this graphic organizer to construct relationships among parts of a whole, to show divisions, or to show relative size of the pieces of the pie. For example, in a physical education class, students can determine the percentage of time a football team spends on offense and defense compared with their opponents. They can also identify how much of the offensive time is spent executing passing plays and how much in running plays.

KWL

This graphic organizer was originated by Donna Ogle in 1986 (What do you *know* about the topic? What do you *want* to know? What have you *learned* about the topic from the lesson or unit?) Students can use this graphic organizer to reflect on their knowledge, to identify deficiencies, and to assess what they have learned. For example, in a chemistry class:

- What do students *know* about the periodic table?
- What do they *want* to know that will help them understand the table?
- What have they *learned* after a lesson or unit on the periodic table.

KDL

What do you *know?* What do you *do?* What have you *learned* about the relationship between knowledge and behavior, or what do you want to learn that will help you align behavior with knowledge? Students can use this graphic organizer to reflect on knowledge, identify behaviors, and evaluate incongruencies and/or connections between knowledge and behavior. For example, in a health class, what do students know about the importance and benefits of a personal fitness program? Do they exercise regularly? What do they want to learn that can help them get started exercising or exercise more consistently?

PMI

What are the *pluses* (positives)? What are the *minuses* (negatives)? What else is *interesting* or *intriguing?* Students can use a PMI chart to evaluate content, data, or results. For example, in a health class, what is positive about managed health care? What is negative about managed health care? What are some interesting points about managed health care?

Right Angle

What are the *facts?* What are your *thoughts, opinions, feelings, expectations, predictions* about those facts? Students can use this graphic organizer to identify facts beside the horizontal line and to associate their thoughts and feelings about the facts below the vertical line. Students are asked to distinguish fact from hearsay or conjecture, to link facts with their thoughts about the facts and the resulting feelings and reactions to the facts, to change the direction of their thinking about the facts, and to use facts to predict. For example, in a history class, students can list facts about land mine use around the world, identify how they feel about land mine use, and predict what they think will eventually happen with the use of land mines. And in a technology class, students can describe the current state of technology and privacy, how they feel about individual privacy rights, and how they think technology and privacy rights will be resolved.

Staff Development: Pathway to a New Paradigm

Bringing about a community of learners necessitates a school culture of professional development. The successful transition to block scheduling is dependent upon a shift in teachers' perceptual orientation, or understanding of the world around them. Those whose worldview is relatively rigid and inflexible tend to gravitate to a lecture-style approach. Consequently, such teachers may need more intensive training than those holding more fluid, dynamic, and flexible views who are more easily adapted to brain-compatible teaching approaches suited to the block (Caine and Caine 1997). An approach to teacher development that supports substantive professional growth will help bring about a paradigm shift by the entire school community. Professional development that focuses on brain-compatible instructional strategies is an important component of best practice within an extended time block.

A RAND study recently concluded that "new teaching strategies can require as much as 50 hours of instruction, practice, and coaching before teachers become comfortable with them," while another study concluded that fifty *days* were needed (U.S. Department of Education 1994). Canady and Rettig (1995) suggest a *minimum* of five (optimally ten) full-day workshops where teachers transitioning into a block schedule can learn teaching and classroom management techniques. In addition, they need to interact with and model teachers experienced in teaching in the block. At any rate, such "sustained periods of professional development" (Cushman 1995) are nowhere more imperative than when teaching in the block. Happily, another study of education reform efforts conducted in 1994 found that "allowing schools and districts to reconfigure schedules to provide time for collaboration and learning is possibly the most cost-efficient means of providing at least some of the time required" for teachers to learn how to improve student achievement (O'Day, Goertz, and Floden 1995, 57).

It is important to remember that instructional time need not be sacrificed on the altar of staff development. "Ironically, the change to block scheduling that has generated a need for new teaching strategies can also provide extended time during the school day for staff development" (Canady and Rettig 1995, 14). Two- to fifteen-day "mini-terms" can be built into a school year in which teachers alternate staff development and instruction assignments as discussed in chapter 2. In addition, see Figures 4.8 "Staff Development in a Semester System" and 4.9 "Staff Development in a Trimester System."

Staff Development in a Semester System

First Half of First Semester	Break		Second Half of First Semester	Break		First Half of Second Semester	Break	
	Group 1—Staff Development			Group 2—Staff Development			Group 3—Staff Development	
	Group 2 & 3—Enrichment Courses			Group 1 & 3—Enrichment Courses			Group 1 & 2—Enrichment Courses	

Figure 4.8

Staff Development in a Trimester System

First Trimester	Break	Second Trimester	Break	Third Trimester
	Group 1—Staff Development		Group 2—Staff Development	
	Group 2 Plus Outside Sources—Enrichment Courses		Group 1 Plus Outside Sources—Enrichment Courses	

Figure 4.9

The various brain-compatible techniques and strategies discussed in this chapter come together in Sample Four-Phase Lesson Plan #4. It is designed as a culminating lesson of a unit on population trends and changes. The curriculum connection includes foreign language, mathematics (statistics), technology, and health. If teachers work in teams that include both a foreign language and health teacher, they can team-teach this lesson. The foreign language selected can be one students take in school or one that is spoken by students in school. The foreign language focus is to strengthen vocabulary and to better understand foreign cultures. The health focus for this lesson is nutrition; however, any health issue could be addressed, such as diseases, accidents, lifestyle choices (such as alcohol consumption and smoking), or health-care availability. Just about any content area can be taught in a foreign language, allowing students to increase their language fluency while working on a different content area.

Sample Four-Phase Lesson Plan

Gender, Age, and Pyramids–Only Your Sarcophagus Knows for Sure!

Level: Middle

Curriculum Integration: Social Science, Mathematics, Foreign Language (Spanish), Technology, and Health

Multiple Intelligences

- ☑ Bodily/Kinesthetic
- ☐ Interpersonal
- ☐ Intrapersonal
- ☑ Logical/Mathematical

- ☐ Musical
- ☐ Naturalist
- ☑ Verbal/Linguistic
- ☑ Visual/Spatial

Content Standards

SOCIAL STUDIES

Understands that culture and experience influence people's perceptions of places and regions

Understands global development and environmental issues

Understands the forces of cooperation and conflict that shape the divisions of Earth's surface

Understands the patterns and networks of economic interdependence on Earth's surface

Understands the changes that occur in the meaning, use, distribution and importance of resources

HEALTH

Knows the availability and effective use of health services, products, and information

Knows environmental and external factors that affect individual and community health

Understands essential concepts about nutrition and diet

Understands how eating properly can help reduce health risks

FOREIGN LANGUAGE

Uses the target language to engage in conversations, express feelings and emotions, and exchange opinions and information

TECHNOLOGY

Evaluates electronic sources of information

MATHEMATICS

Understands and applies basic and advanced concepts of statistics and data analysis

INQUIRE PHASE
25 MINUTES

Inquire Activity

Objective: Students discuss their population pyramid homework assignment in Spanish and synthesize the information they gathered.

ATTEND

A population pyramid is a graph that shows patterns of population change by using four values:

- total country population by decade or five-year interval
- percent of population that is male for each decade or five-year interval
- percent of population that is female for each decade or five-year interval
- year of birth of each decade or five-year interval

See Figure 4.10 "Population Pyramid."

Picking up on the lesson presented the previous day from which students completed a population pyramid for homework, the teacher . . .

- Pairs students and directs their attention by beginning the following dialogue in Spanish:

  Think about all the information you collected for your population pyramid assignment. What are some key words that relate in some way to your pyramids? Please share them with the class using Spanish.

Population Pyramid

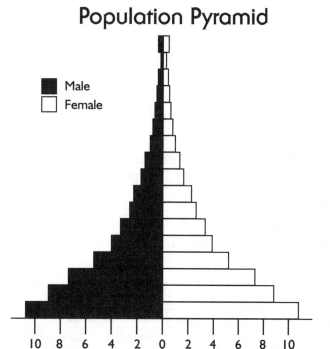

Figure 4.10

EXPERIENCE: TODAY, POPULATION PYRAMIDS; TOMORROW THE WORLD!

The teacher . . .

- writes student responds in Spanish and in English on the chalk board or pyramid chart paper. Words students suggest may include

hombre: man	*familia:* family
mujer: woman	*generación:* generation
gente: people	*piramide:* pyramid
decenio: decade	*por ciento:* percent
abuelos: grandparents	*joven:* young
ancianidad: old age	*muerte:* death
vecino: neighbor	*cuarenta:* forties

- Corrects or clarifies any mispronunciations.

Student pairs . . .

- Create a statement regarding population pyramids using the above words.
- Volunteer to share their statements in both English and Spanish.
- Repeat the process two or three times using different words from the list each time.

- Review their homework projects with each other and share the results of their population pyramids with the class.

REFLECT

Students . . .

- Place their completed population pyramid homework assignment in their working portfolio
- Add this latest entry on their portfolio's contents sheet.
- Look through portfolio entries to see if something needs to be removed or reworked.
- Use a portfolio assessment rubric to evaluate their portfolios. See Figure 4.11 "Portfolio Evaluation Rubric."

Portfolio Evaluation Rubric				
Qualities Evaluated	**LEVEL OF WORK**			
	Excellent	Accomplished	Developing	Beginning
Organization	Deliberate and effective Includes up-to-date contents page	Organized Has contents page	Organizational structure not readily apparent Contents page is outdated and/or missing entries	Disorganized No contents page
Presentation	Dynamic and unique	Effort evident	Some effort evident	Little effort evident
Entries Included	Evidence growth and superior work	A variety of entries that demonstrate growth	Lack an apparent rationale for inclusion	Few entries or shows little or no growth

Figure 4.11

GATHER PHASE
25 MINUTES

Gather Activity

Objective: Students evaluate a new population pyramid.

ATTEND

The teacher asks . . .

- Based on what you have learned about creating population pyramids, what do you think you can determine by merely looking at the pyramid?

Students . . .

- Are assigned to one of five small, expert groups, with the direction to evaluate the same population pyramid but with each group focusing on one of the following:
  - demographic transition stage (1st, 2nd, or 3rd)
  - health issues
  - economics
  - historical trends and events
  - type(s) of government.
- Identify details of the population pyramid based on patterns and implied statistics.
- Prepare a pyramid chart of their expert assessment in their expert groups.
- Stay in their expert groups, rotate from pyramid chart to pyramid chart, evaluating each pyramid chart, adding insights or raising questions about interpretations.
- After three or four rotations, groups return to their original expert pyramid charts to reflect on the additions or questions and refine their pyramid charts. Groups share their expert pyramid charts with the rest of the class.

EXPERIENCE: "GRAPHIC DEMOGRAPHICS"

Students . . .

- Prepare a graphic organizer (concept map, matrix, fishbone, etc.) of key points from all five topics for use in evaluating population pyramids.

- Share their graphic organizers with other groups and the class.
- Place completed organizers in their working portfolio.

REFLECT

The teacher asks the following questions . . .

- What information can be determined from evaluating a population pyramid?
- What new insights have you gained about the formal process of evaluating population pyramids?
- What will you remember to do the next time you are asked to interpret population pyramids or other graphs and tables?

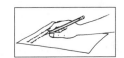

PROCESS PHASE
25 MINUTES

Process Activity

Objective: Students select a Spanish-speaking country and create a population pyramid based on information they gather about the country.

ATTEND

The teacher calls student attention to the next task by asking the following questions . . .

- In what part(s) of the world do people speak Spanish?
- Why have those places adopted that language?
- Does the language commonly spoken in a place have an effect on the culture, or vice versa?

EXPERIENCE: "SPANNING THE GLOBE"

Students in small groups . . .

- Choose a specific Spanish-speaking country (Bolivia, Cuba, Mexico, Puerto Rico, Spain, etc.) and determine what kind of information they want to gather about that country.
- Jigsaw resources to search for specific information on the Internet they can use to create a population pyramid. (See Appendix.)

- Share their pyramids with two or three other groups.
- Submit their pyramids to the teacher, who selects a few pyramids to facilitate a class discussion on the information presented in the pyramids.

REFLECT

The teacher asks the following questions:

- What interesting facts did you learn about the country you researched?
- Which sources were most helpful in finding the information you needed?
- How did you find those sources?
- How could you help other students who are having difficulty finding information they need, regardless of the topic?

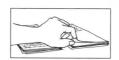

APPLY PHASE
15 MINUTES

Apply Activity

Objective: Students consider nutritional factors that can influence population density.

ATTEND

The teacher asks . . .

- What kind of food do you typically eat for breakfast?
- How healthy do you think your breakfast is? Tell a partner.

Students . . .

- List all the breakfast foods they eat and/or that are typical for persons in their community.
- Evaluate the foods, using a nutrition resource guide, for (a) calories of fat, carbohydrate, and protein, (b) vitamins and minerals, and (c) nutrient density.

EXPERIENCE: "BREAKFAST OF CHAMPIONS"

The teacher . . .

- Leads a discussion on the role of nutrition in longevity, diseases, health problems, growth and development, etc.

- Assigns a homework project in which students select two persons from the following list to interview to ask what breakfast foods they ate when they were 13 or 14 years old:
    - Their parents or another adult the age of their parents, and
    - Their grandparents or someone the age of their grandparents
    - Someone who grew up in a Spanish-speaking country and is the age of their parents or older.

Students will . . .

- Analyze the nutritional content of the foods and compare/contrast the differences among the three generations —
    - (1) their own breakfast analysis
    - (2) their parents, and
    - (3) their grandparents.

The teacher, in conjunction with the class . . .

- Creates a four-level rubric that further defines the assignment and is used later to evaluate their homework assignment. An example of such a rubric is Figure 4.12 "Four-Level Homework Evaluation Rubric"

REFLECT

The teacher asks the following questions:

- What are five things you learned about the many factors and circumstances that can influence a population both positively and negatively?
- What are some reasons governments and health organizations monitor a population by organizing details in graphs like a population pyramid?
- If you were the president of a Third World country, what would be the first thing(s) you would do to improve the quality of life for your people?

Four-Level Homework Evaluation Rubric

Qualities Evaluated	LEVEL OF WORK			
	A (4)	B (3)	C (2)	Not Yet (1)
Analysis of Nutritional Content	A wide variety of foods were appropriately analyzed, taking into account several factors	Derived from only two nutritional factors	Derived from one nutritional factor	Foods listed but not evaluated for nutritional content
Data Collection	Surveyed two or more persons from each of three generations	Surveyed one person from each of three genera-tions	Surveyed two generations	Surveyed self only
Organization and Presentation of Data	Used appropriate words in Spanish Supplied a carefully drawn and accurate graph that accounts for all variables in the foods and the persons inter-viewed	Supplied an accurate and neatly drawn graph	Graph supplied was insufficient to represent all the variables	Raw data only, no graph
Comments:				

Figure 4.12

CHAPTER 5

ASSESSMENT

MEASURING ACHIEVEMENT AND GROWTH IN THE BLOCK

Authentic classroom assessments provide teachers with a repertoire of tools to measure student growth. ...[T]eachers need to create vivid, colorful, and true moving pictures of a student as he or she develops and grows over the course of a year.

—Kay Burke 1994, *xxi*

The Right Stuff

One of the assessment tools that will continue to be used is objective testing. Practical alternatives and sound arguments exist, however, for a new brain-compatible and authentic means of measuring student achievement. Grant Wiggins (1989) suggests that educators should actually teach to the test, but the tests to which they teach need to be very different from what they are now. The *right* kind of assessment is central to the learning process and engages students in real-life situations and applications. Kay Burke defines assessment as the "process of gathering evidence" (Burke 1994, *xvi*). If this is so, then clearly, the more diverse the sources of evidence, the more accurate the picture one can create of student strengths, abilities, and learning differences. In addition, by addressing assessment *during* the instructional-design stage—what Ferrar and McTighe (1996) and Wiggins (1989) call "backward planning"—the entire curricular process is shaped for the better. More brain-compatible assessments actually promote the instructional process like those in the *process phase* of a four-phase lesson plan. Conversely, the practice of teaching to the rigidity of the conventional standardized test with its set of mysterious "correct" answers is outdated and counterproductive. Figure 5.1 illustrates the differences between standardized test formats and their brain-compatible counterparts.

Surface knowledge, fact-based rather than context-based learning (the type most often measured by standardized tests), "does not prepare students to solve complex problems and apply the knowledge to unexpected and complex real-life situations" (Caine, Caine, and Crowell 1994, 47). What is called for is the development within students of dynamic thinking that can adapt to changing circumstances and conditions. Complex thinking is a journey into ambiguous, messy arenas of facts and opinions, which calls for very different kinds of assessment tools. Fogarty and Stoehr (1995) offer the "tri-assessment model," which suggests a combination of three approaches to assessment:

- Traditional test and quiz assessment
- Gathering samples of actual ongoing work into a portfolio
- Observations of students actually carrying out processes, demonstrations, and performances

The key to the tri-assessment model is varying the types of assessment a teacher uses, much the same way a teacher needs to vary instructional strategies. (See chapters 3 and 4.) Evidence from various assessment approaches

STANDARDIZED TESTS vs. BRAIN-COMPATIBLE ASSESSMENT

Standardized Testing	*Brain-Compatible Assessment*
• results based on a mythical standard or norm, which requires that a certain percentage of children fail	• establishes an environment where each child has the opportunity to succeed
• pressures teachers to narrow their curriculum so that they can specifically concentrate on the test material	• allows teachers to develop meaningful curricula and assess within the context of that program
• emphasizes a single-instance assessment, which has no relation to the learning taking place in the classroom	• assessment is ongoing throughout the unit of study and provides an accurate picture of student achievement
• focuses on errors and mistakes rather than on what has been accomplished	• puts the emphasis on student strengths rather than weaknesses
• focuses too much importance on single sets of data (i.e. test scores) in making educational decisions	• provides multiple sources of evaluation that give an in-depth view of student progress
• treats all students in a uniform way	• treats each student as a unique human being
• discriminates against some students because of cultural background and learning style	• provides the opportunity to eliminate cultural bias and gives everyone an equal chance to succeed
• regards instruction and assessment as separate activities	• regards instruction and assessment as being a single, integrated activity
• answers are final, there is no opportunity for reflection or revision	• engages the student in a continual process of self-reflection, learning, and feedback, as well as revision
• focuses on the "right" answer without regard for understanding	• deals with comprehension and the learning process as much as the final product
• inexpensive and easy to administer and grade	• more difficult to achieve consistent, objective scoring results
• often provides results that can be simplified to a single numerical score	• data cannot easily be simplified as a single number
• easy to compare and contrast different populations of students	• difficult to compare different student populations

Figure 5.1

Adapted from *Brain-Compatible Assessments* by Diane Ronis. ©1999 by SkyLight Training and Publishing, Inc. Reprinted with permission of SkyLight Professional Development, Arlington Heights, IL.

provides a multidimensional view—a "moving" picture, so to speak—that more accurately depicts a student's knowledge, understanding, and capability than can any one type alone. In addition, higher levels of thinking are best measured by authentic, less-traditional forms of assessment. Figure 5.2 "Forms of Assessment" suggests the benefits and characteristics of three forms of assessment.

Forms of Assessment

	Traditional Assessment	Portfolio Assessment	Performance Assessment
Definition	Written summaries of learnings	A collection of work samples from a unit or a semester or a year	Direct observation of a student's performance
Time Component	Periodically	Contiually add evidence	Toward the end of a lesson or unit
Benefits	• Easy to grade • Answers are often right or wrong • Displays knowledge of details	• Shows growth and develop-ment	• Focuses on what a student does, or on skills a student can demonstrate
Intelligences	• Verbal/Linguistic • Logical/Mathematical • Visual/Spatial	• Visual/Spatial • Intrapersonal • Verbal/Linguistic • Logical/Mathematical • Interpersonal	• Visual/Spatial • Bodily/Kinesthetic • Verbal/Linguistic • Logical/Mathematical • Interpersonal • Musical/Rhythmic • Naturalist
Assessment Tool	Answer sheet • Graphic Organizers • Journals	Rubric • Standards • Criteria • Indicators • Checklist • Graphic Organizers • Reflections on Portfolio Contents	Rubric • Standards • Criteria • Indicators • Checklist

Figure 5.2

Adapted from *Best Practices for the Learner-Centered Classroom* by Robin Fogarty. ©1995 SkyLight Training and Publishing Inc. Reprinted with permission of SkyLight Professional Development, Arlington Heights, IL.

Caught in the Act of Learning: Authentic Assessment

As discussed in previous chapters, there is a necessity for students to perceive a connection between the curriculum and their real lives. Without some kind of relationship, there is little motivation to become involved with course content. The same can be said of the form of assessment used to determine what a student has learned. It is not that quizzes, multiple-choice, and standardized tests are ineffective; rather, it is that these forms are not enough to give witness to what students "know." Alternative, authentic forms of assessments can be utilized to gain a clear understanding of student learning.

Authentic assessments are those evaluative tools that are relevant and connected to real-life situations. In addition, they recognize the myriad of different student learning styles and provide repeated and various opportunities for students to demonstrate what they have learned. The important connection between "authentic" classroom learning tasks and "authentic" assessment techniques needs to exist. Using the first without the second runs counter to common sense. In the same vein, if educators are facilitating the acquisition of higher-level thinking skills, then the assessment itself needs to be rigorous enough to measure the depth of understanding such an approach brings about (Burke 1994).

Authentic assessments are an excellent system for providing students with a natural and immediate feedback loop. Students using an authentic assessment tool are aware of the performance requirements as they rehearse; they are assessed according to the very requirements they have been rehearsing, and then they are provided feedback regarding how closely they have met the requirements. With the feedback that is part of every assessment tool, students can make immediate alterations in their performance or emerging understanding. Feedback that is specific and immediate is essential to ensure that knowledge or skills are integrated into an appropriate schema and successfully stored in long-term memory. Without consistent and effective feedback, mistakes or "bugs" may be rehearsed over and over again, creating an inappropriate schema stored in long-term memory. Students who have created a malformed schema may never realize their mistake. If and when a misunderstanding or mispatterning is realized, students may have to exert an exhaustive effort to modify their schema. In addition, the timing of feedback needs to be consistent and immediate. Delays in feedback are not harmful as long as students are provided feedback at a time when they can recall their performance clearly and accurately. Authentic assessment tools are ideal for providing students with immediate, consistent, and accurate feedback.

A pleasant by-product of authentic assessment is the emotional context in which the assessment takes place. Emotion plays a central role not only in learning and memory but also in the conditions under which a person is best able to recall and apply information. Because authentic assessment is ongoing and an integral part of the instructional process, the test anxiety often associated with more traditional forms of assessment, most notably the standardized test, is not present. Students are relatively free from stress and are better able to demonstrate what they know.

Longer class times permit authentic assessment in ways that shorter class periods cannot. In a traditional fifty-minute class period, there is often barely enough time for teachers to impart the *who, what,* and *when* of the curricular material. Larger blocks of time allow teachers to guide students to the *why* and *how* elements of the learning equation. Students have time to internalize the material and demonstrate that they know how to apply the material to real-life tasks and situations. Remembering Burke's (1994) definition of assessment as the process of gathering evidence; the question for teaching in the block becomes "What other methods can teachers use to obtain evidence of student understanding?" Skillful teachers expand the variety of assessment forms they use whenever possible. Employing conferences, graphic organizers, journals, logs, observation checklists, portfolios, and rubrics provides teachers *and* the students themselves with evidence that learning is occurring. Each is discussed below.

Conferences allow opportunities for the teacher to meet one on one with a student or a student team. While other class teams are working on projects or other tasks, the teacher can meet with students and verbally check on what learning is going on. Block scheduling offers the kind of multitask lesson flow that permits teacher-student conferencing.

Graphic Organizers are visual tools to help students organize and process a great deal of information. (For a more detailed discussion, see chapter 4.)

Journals and Logs are ongoing writing opportunities that allow students to write and reflect upon ongoing learning. Journals are open-ended and contain more personal reflections than logs, which are used for more content-specific reflections, such as thoughts or observations about a science experiment, Internet search, field trip, or service learning experience. In addition, journals and logs offer the type of low-intensity activity essential to pulsed learning.

Observation Checklists are lists of specific criteria a teacher uses to determine a students level of mastery of an activity or concept. Such checklists can include performance criteria related to the following:

General Observations	Specific Criteria
• Social skills • Group dynamics • Presentation skills • Laboratory procedures • Steps in the writing and/or researching process	• Disagrees with ideas not the person • Encourages fellow students on his or her team • Speaks clearly and at a moderate rate • Uses appropriate visual tools while presenting • Gathers all the lab material before beginning the lab procedure • Documents each research source

Performance criteria are usually derived by the teacher, a teacher team, or a department from the broader content standards.

Portfolios are collections and samples of student work chosen by the teacher and the student to represent the student's growth and achievement. Portfolios are not just snapshots but moving pictures that illuminate achievement and growth over time. Like journals and logs, portfolio collection and reflection time are low-intensity activities that, in addition to their use in the assessment process, also serve as counterpoints to higher intensity activities. In its simplist form, the portfolio process has three stages: collection, selection, and reflection (Fogarty 1997a).

- *Collection.* Creating the work that may be appropriately placed in the portfolio or gathering artifacts or exhibits that add dimension to an entry or to the overall presentation of the portfolio.
- *Selection.* Determining what materials to include in the portfolio. It is important to note that not only "perfect" work is included. Work that reflects progress and illuminates the process of learning is not only appropriate but necessary to draw a full picture of achievement.

- *Reflection.* Like other activities, portfolio entries are thought about and looked back upon, which requires time to think about the content's purpose and meaning.

Rubrics use specific performance criteria to evaluate the level of student performance on a task or activity. Rubrics give clear guidelines to the student of what "good" and "good enough" look like before they undertake a task. The teacher then uses the rubric to ascertain student achievement. The student isn't left guessing what the teacher is looking for.

Figure 5.3 shows an open "Rubric Template" that teachers may use themselves or with students when constructing such an assessment tool. The column on the far left side of the template is where performance elements such as communication, organization, teamwork, accuracy, originality, and presentation can be listed. The person or persons constructing the rubric generally selects one or two labels for each performance level ("accomplished" and "B," for example). Students may want to use more trendy or informal language to label the levels. Teachers need to make sure the terms are positive ones such as (from lowest to highest level):

First Base—Second Base—Third Base—Home Run!

Apprentice—Expert—Master

Needs more thought—Awesome!

Rubric Template				
	Performance Levels			
Essential Elements of Performance	Proficient Excellent/ Advanced "A" "4"	Accomplished Good "B" "3"	Basic Acceptable "C" "2"	Novice Not Yet "D" "1"
	Specific Performance Criteria ⟶			

Figure 5.3

The template shows four levels, but rubrics can have as few as two levels—acceptable and unacceptable for example. Two-level rubrics are often constructed to evaluate journal entries. The specific performance criteria fill in the rest of the grid. It is perhaps easiest to begin with what the best possible work would look like. At the highest level, the criteria are challenging and akin to what may have been formerly considered "extra credit." It is only by going the extra mile, so to speak, that students can attain the highest level.

Figure 5.4 directs the reader to other figures in this book that illustrate the various assessment tools discussed above as part of the four-phase lesson plans at the end of chapters 1 though 5.

Evaluation Tools Modeled	
Tool	**As Illustrated in Figures**
Four-Level Rubric	2.8, 4.12, 5.3 (template), 5.5
Group Presentation Rubric	1.5
Teacher Observation	3.6
Portfolio Evaluation Rubric	4.11
Student Self-Assessment	3.9

Figure 5.4

Students who underperform on traditional tests can communicate their mastery of material through projects, performances, or demonstrations. Further, authentic assessment is perhaps the best chance for students to show "how they are smart" in terms of their own unique development of the intelligences. This presents a real challenge to teachers accustomed to working within the confines of the traditional time and assessment structure. Therefore, ongoing staff development is a necessary ingredient of successful block scheduling.

Testing Matters

For better or worse, schools and their programs are often judged by the outcomes of standardized tests. Testing is a fact of life. While standardized tests will no doubt remain an educational constant, how schools and teachers relate to the tests will have a huge impact on their students. In an alternative scheduling context, the question of standardized testing is all the more pronounced. The success of alternative scheduling is often judged by the performance of students in the block relative to their peers learning under a traditional schedule (Benton-Kupper 1999). Perhaps the two biggest perceived challenges to the efficacy of a block schedule are scope and recency of materials covered. "If the focus remains on surface learning and low-level recall, then the recency of exposure is critical!" (Rettig and Canady 1996, 10). But if the material is covered in depth, greater retention for longer periods can be achieved. Teachers experienced in the block report they can discern little educational significance between the difference in retention of students who recently completed a class over those students with greater time lapses between courses. So, once again, the question appears not so much to be one of the assessment or testing process but one of curricular material and instructional approaches.

The greatest predictor of student performance is what actually takes place in the classroom, whether it takes place in the block or within a conventional schedule. Students taught with strategies that tap into their long-term memory have a better chance to recall material on standardized tests than they would if their short-term memory were the focus. (See chapter 1 for a discussion of memory.) "Not surprisingly, students given instruction aimed at conceptual understanding do better on skills tests than students drilled on the skills directly" (Carpenter and others 1988). In addition to teaching to long-term memory, teachers need to employ the best practices in structuring extended class time. If teachers fail to use the time in the block efficiently, a decrease in standardized test scores can result.

By postponing higher-order thinking goals, skills remediation classes have a deletenous effect on the standarized test scores of students placed in these classes. Low-achieving students suffer most from a proficiency-driven curriculum (measured by standardized tests) because they are consigned indefinitely to dull and repetitive skills instruction that does not enable them to grasp underlying concepts (Levin, Glass, and Meister 1987). Luckily, brain-compatible learning approaches can have a dramatic impact even on students who have previously been labeled "low achieving." When instructional approaches are varied, when the curriculum content is made relevant and applicable to real-life situations, learning moves from mere rote memorization to deeply internalized, usable information. When this occurs, the material can be retained far longer than previously thought possible. Longer class times allow teachers more occasions to discern how well the material is being absorbed and to decide whether any reteaching strategies are needed to enable students to better grasp the material (Fitzgerald 1996).

Iron Out the "Forgetting Curve"

Some schools teaching in the block prepare their students for standardized tests by scheduling *structured review sessions*. Such sessions are scheduled three or four weeks before the tests are given. Their purpose is to help students recall the significant details needed for the test. If the original class work has emphasized the frameworks and the concepts, then the review sessions need only remind the students of these frameworks and concepts and then help the students get on top of the details again. On the other hand, if the original class work neglected sense-making frameworks and concepts, then it is as if the students are just beginning to absorb the details needed for the tests. This will make preparing for the standardized tests doubly difficult (College Boards Online1999).

Extended time formats permit the teacher to spend time teaching the concepts and the overall frameworks of the material being presented. Probing questions that help students make connections to other material can be just the connections needed to push the material into long-term memory.

While student performance on standardized tests isn't the purpose of teaching, brain-compatible teaching methodologies that lay out frameworks and concepts as containers for crucial facts and information greatly enable peak student performance on such tests (Burke 1992). The more brain-compatible the structured review sessions are, the more powerful and long-lasting their effect will be. Students working within a system that harnesses the power of cooperative learning, recognizes multiple intelligences, facilitates the expansion of higher-order thinking skills, and provides adequate time for learning and metacognition retain information for use on standardized tests and beyond.

Tests Are Changing

Today, some standardized tests are very different from the simple multiple-choice tests of years ago (Burke 1992). Thinking and the ability to transfer and connect information are increasingly becoming part of standardized tests. Because the tests are changing, it is even more important than ever that teaching in the block emphasize concepts, frameworks, higher-order thinking skills, and applications to real life. Details are important. Discrete pieces of information will continue to be tested; however, much more is demanded of students in the real world than recollection of isolated bits of information. The brain-compatible pedagogy that alternative scheduling facilitates and encourages is well-suited to meet the rigorous demands society and the economy place on the educational system.

Measure Up

The ultimate reason and perhaps the only valid reason for implementing a program such as alternative block scheduling is because it has a positive impact on student achievement. Possibly the easiest way to "judge" (or at least the most frequently used way) student success and program success is testing. So naturally, the first trial block scheduling must undergo is how it fares under the glare of standardized testing. Studies have shown that students in the block have fared as well on such tests as their counterparts in traditionally scheduled classes (Baylis 1983). Several studies have found that both student conduct (attendance, attention, and morale) and academic performance (content mastery, post-test versus pre-test gains, and standardized test scores) are improved when block scheduling is instituted (Baylis 1983, Carroll 1994, Benton-Kupper 1999).

Assessment in Four-Phase Lesson and Unit Design

When teachers use the Four-Phase Lesson design with its repeated "attend-experience-reflect" cycle they have an automatic, built-in format for providing students with thoughtful feedback in the form of authentic assessment. The design provides teachers with a structure for helping students process their learning, evaluate their respective levels of performance, and use authentic assessment as a natural part of the learning process.

The assessment process is integral to the learning process. Students need to engage in defining the performance criteria and working toward attaining high standards. Authentic assessment helps students achieve "excellence" because they know in advance what it looks like from the rubric or other format for the criteria.

Sample Four-Phase Lesson Plan # 5 is a structured review lesson in preparation for students taking a college advanced-placement (AP) test and, as stated above, is a method for "ironing out," or recalling information previously stored in long-term memory. *Science Schmience or Who Framed Sir Isaac Newton?* is offered here as a sample of what could be included in a unit taught in a mini session (see chapter 2's discussion of yearly schedules). The purposes of the lesson are to assist students in remembering important information, identifying ways to associate the information, and familiarizing themselves with the AP test question format. The curriculum connection is science. The AP European history teacher may want to invite one or more of the science teachers (physics, psychology, chemistry, biology, physiology) to act as a resource person during this lesson. While science was selected as the focus of this lesson, the focus could be any of the broad topics covered in AP European history such as art, music, literature, economics, government, war, or any other applicable topic.

Notice how students manipulate the course content in a variety of ways. Students do all of the talking and discussing during this lesson. Since students are reviewing in preparation for a major test, it is critical for them to share their knowledge and insights with each other, to practice saying things they might actually write, and to hear how others have connected the information to clarify their own understanding and to remember details and concepts.

Sample Four-Phase Lesson Plan

Science Schmience or Who Framed Sir Isaac Newton?

Level: Secondary

Curriculum Integration: European History and Science

Multiple Intelligences

- ☑ Bodily/Kinesthetic
- ☑ Interpersonal
- ☐ Intrapersonal
- ☑ Logical/Mathematical

- ☐ Musical
- ☐ Naturalist
- ☑ Verbal/Linguistic
- ☑ Visual/Spacial

Content Standards

WORLD HISTORY (EUROPEAN)

Understands major trends, technological advances, cultural innovations, and political, social, and cultural redefinitions in Europe from 4000 BCE to 20th century

Understands the impact of scientific and technological innovations on 20th century society

Understands major reasons for the great disparities between scientifically advanced industrialized nations and developing nations

SCIENCE

Understands the nature of scientific knowledge

Understands the scientific enterprise

INQUIRE PHASE
20 MINUTES

Inquire Activity Option A

Objective: To recall events from European history and arrange them in chronological order.

ATTEND

The teacher begins a dialogue in the following way . . .

- Today is a review of European history from the scientists' point of view.
- Think about all the scientific advances and issues that have had an impact on the political, economic, social, religious, intellectual, and artistic development of Europe.
- Discuss some of your thoughts with a classmate next to you.

EXPERIENCE: "HUMAN TIMELINE"

Each student . . .

- Independently chooses an event from European history.
- Draws a picture or other visual representation of the event on a 5- by 7-inch card or blank sheet of paper.
- Secures their completed card or paper to the front of their shirt with tape.
- Moves about the room to find one or more other students who have depicted the same event or an event that influenced or was influenced by their event.
- Lines up in chronological order with those they have identified as being somehow related to their topic.
- Discusses their event within their small group and then shares the events they depicted with the rest of the class.

REFLECT

Students . . .

- Write in their metacognitive journals about their perceptions of how recent scientific discoveries have impacted today's culture, society, and government.

Inquire Activity Option B

Objective: Students recall and relate historical events having to do with science and the course of European history.

ATTEND

Teachers ask the following questions to start a class discussion . . .

- Do you think you have a good memory? Why or why not?
- Is a good memory important in an age when computers contain trillions of bits of information? Why or why not?

EXPERIENCE: "WHERE SCIENCE AND HISTORY COLLIDE"

Students . . .

- Working alone, list every issue or event that comes to mind related to European history and science.
- Compare their lists in pairs or triads.

The teacher . . .

- Leads a whole-class discussion following each brainstorm and small-group sharing.
- Repeats the process two or three times.

REFLECT

The teacher asks the class . . .

- What reminders were there for you during the Human Timeline activities?
- What did you hear that became clearer, made more sense, or introduced new connections to you?
- What can you do to remember this information?

GATHER PHASE
25 MINUTES

Gather Activity Option A

Objective: Students "gather," from other students and their own memory, specific elements of European history that were affected by scientific discoveries.

ATTEND

The teacher begins a class discussion that will introduce the students to the experience . . .

- In our next experience you will have to think like a detective.
- Does anybody know what *deductive reasoning* means?
- When would it be used? And by whom?
- If I told you that *inductive reasoning* uses the opposite method of determining information of deductive reasoning, what do you think the term means?

EXPERIENCE: "ROVING INVESTIGATORS"

The teacher . . .

- Writes one person, place, event, or issue on a 3- by 5-inch card, filling out as many cards as there are ideas generated in the *inquire* phase (at least one for every student).
- Randomly places one card on the back of each student without the student knowing what item is on his or her back.

Students . . .

- Meander around the room asking "yes or no" or "true or false" questions of each other to determine the entry on their backs.
- May not give hints and must answer truthfully.
- Determine who or what is on their backs, then turn in their cards to the teacher and receive a different card.
- Continue investigating until every card is identified or until time is up.

Gather Activity Option B

Objective: Students design memory aids.

ATTEND

The teacher asks the following questions to begin a class discussion...

- When you were younger, how did you memorize spelling words?
- Do you or did you go about studying for a test on the plot and meaning of a novel differently than you would have studied for a spelling test?

EXPERIENCE: "LEFT TO THEIR OWN DEVICES"

Students . . .

- In groups of three or four, design mnemonics and visuals, write lyrics to familiar tunes, or invent other ways to help them remember details about the names, places, and events on the cards.

REFLECT
"Talking Circles"

Students . . .

- Stand in two concentric circles, with half the students on the inside circle, the other half on the outside circle.
- Face each other to talk with another student. One circle moves clockwise, while the other moves counterclockwise, moving ahead by one person each time the teacher asks one of the questions below. Each new pair exchanges their answer with the person they encountered on the circle.

The teacher asks . . .

- Of all the information you talked about today, what do you think are the most critical points for you to remember? Why?
- Why is it important to remember this information, beyond taking the AP exam?
- How is your world different today because of what happened in Europe?
- Enough other pertinent questions to complete the circle's cycle once.

PROCESS PHASE
30 MINUTES

Process Activity

Objective: Students create mock AP test questions.

ATTEND

The teacher focuses student attention on the next experience by beginning a discussion . . .

- You are going to create some questions that are AP test quality. What do you think makes an excellent AP question? Share with a partner.

- Look at some sample questions in the AP European history test preparation book. What is the quality of these questions? Share with the class.
- Let's decide what makes a good AP question.

Students and teachers create a checklist for writing test questions.

Students . . .

- Working in groups of three, look through the AP test preparation manual to become familiar with the types of questions posed on the test.
- Determine characteristics of the test questions and the accompanying multiple-choice options.
- Share their findings with the class in order to develop a master set of criteria for use in evaluating the questions the student triads create. The rubric can be used for student self-evaluation, as refined directions for the activity, and as the instrument with which the students are evaluated on the experience.)

EXPERIENCE: "MOCK QUESTIONS"

Students . . .

- Working in the same groups and using the established criteria (see Figure 5.5) generate mock questions with a focus on science (three multiple-choice questions that include answer options and one essay question).
- Join another group and answer each other's test questions. Answers are discussed and groups give feedback to each other on the quality of the questions they created.
- Move to a different group and repeat the process one or two more times.
- Submit their test questions to the teacher.

The teacher . . .

- Randomly selects questions to ask the whole class.
- Facilitates a discussion on each question, reinforcing appropriate responses and eliciting multiple answers.
- Evaluates each group's questions using the rubric.

REFLECT

The teacher asks the following questions, prompting student discussion...

- What do you think makes a good test question?
- How will knowing how good test questions are written help you be a better test taker?
- What procedure should you follow when answering multiple-choice and essay questions to improve the quality of your answers?

Mock Question Criteria

	Performance Levels			
	Novice	**Adequate**	**Accomplished**	**Advanced**
Directions Clarity	Difficult to understand	Not entirely clear	Clearly stated	Very clearly and concisely stated
Questions Precision Accuracy Coverage	Did not evidence understanding of the material	Drawn too narrowly or too broadly and/or contained inaccurate references	Careful and accurate	Precise, accurate, and dealt with appropriate and challenging content that sought application of higher-level thinking skills
Options Number provided Length Accuracy	Do not reflect a serious attempt to construct useful and valid options	Provided four options for most Length of options "telegraphed" correct answer Some inaccuracies	Demonstrated understanding of material	Provided five challenging options of equal length for each with a clearly correct answer
Mechanics Spelling Grammar Punctuation	Substantial mechanical errors or repeated misspelling or inconsistently rendering proper names	Some mechanical errors, which in places detracted from question quality	Provided five options for most, some "decoy" options were too obvious and/or answer was too "tricky" Accurate Any errors in mechanics did not significantly detract from question quality	No spelling, grammar or punctuation errors

Figure 5.5

APPLY PHASE
15 MINUTES

Apply Activity

Objective: Students make meaning from the material by making connections between its various elements.

ATTEND

Students . . .

- Identify practical reasons for understanding and remembering information taught in AP European history.
- Write in their personal reflection journal their thoughts on the following questions:
  - What are some legitimate reasons for U.S. high school students to study European history?
  - In what ways are you a different person from the person who began this structured review class?
  - What long-term impact will what you learned about European history and test-taking have on your life?

EXPERIENCE: "CROSS-CONTENT CONNECTIONS"

Students . . .

- In small groups, create a graphic organizer, chart, graph, or other visual that demonstrates the relationship between science and any one of the following as it pertains to European history: visual arts, music, literature, economics, social systems, religion, war, government, or agriculture.
- Prepare to share their visual during the next class.

REFLECT

The teacher poses the following questions . . .

- What is one thing that worries you most about taking the AP exam?
- What would you like to review before you take the exam?
- Who is in the best position to help you prepare for the exam?

Homework Assignment

Students . . .

- Individually review their notes, books, or other sources to add information to their copy of the group visual they have started.

CHAPTER 6

FOUR-PHASE LESSON AND UNIT DESIGN

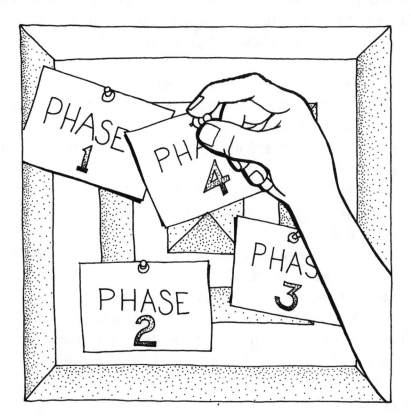

Whereas short lectures and memorization play a part, much more learning takes place when learners are constantly immersed in complex experience; when they process, analyze, and examine this experience for meaning and understanding; and when they constantly relate what they have learned to their own central purposes. When teachers assist students in engaging their own purposes, teachers may find that skill development, with its emphasis on practice, rehearsal, and refinement, becomes more effective. The challenge, therefore, is to fit skills and content to the learner, rather than fit the learner to the curriculum.

—Renate and Geoffrey Caine 1997, 18–19

Inquiring—Gathering—Processing—Applying

The challenge of lesson and unit design is to package curriculum and instruction in a way that both engages students in significant curriculum and stimulates high-level thinking skills. Information and concepts are crucial to student understanding, but just as crucial is the ability to think and to manipulate the information and concepts in ways that demonstrate that the students know how to use and apply the sum of their experience to new situations.

The four-phase lesson and unit design mirrors both the processing model (see Figure 6.1) and the natural progression of the learning process (see Figure 6.2) and is thus both brain-compatible and well-suited to teaching in the block.

Many of the prevailing lesson plan models are not brain-compatible and do not necessarily work well as the organizational structure of a lesson in an extended time format because they:

- Promote one major activity during a lesson rather than several "pulsed activities"
- Do not incorporate brain-compatible activities
- Do not recommend/accommodate mediation, metacognition, or processing
- Reinforce the outmoded concept that the teacher's principle function is to disseminate information
- Lack real problem-solving focus

On the other hand, the four-phase lesson design begins with the *inquire* phase in which questions are posed that the study of the particular curriculum lesson or unit can answer. It is in the first phase that the teacher discovers what prior knowledge is present and hears the questions students would like to see answered throughout the study of the unit. Beginning connections are established here that help the class see the applicability of whatever the content area is. It is in this phase that the teacher helps to generate the kind of interest that can catalyze enough motivation to begin the serious study of the curriculum content.

The remaining three phases are built on Bellanca and Fogarty's (1991) work on the Three-Story Intellect as described in *Blueprints for Thinking in the Cooperative Classroom*. In the *gather* phase, information is presented; data and concepts are researched and amassed; material is observed and described; and stories are summarized or narrated (Bellanca and Fogarty 1991, 88).

The Processing Model and the Four-Phase Lesson Design

What?	Inquire Phase	• What do students know about the lesson content? • What experiences have students had? • What do others know? • What would students like to know?
So what?	Gather Phase	• So what else do students need to know? • So what are the important ideas, knowledge, and skills needed? • So what do students need to do to understand the information or improve their skills?
Now what?	Process Phase	• Now what can students do to remember this information. • Now what activities will clarify the concepts and ensure student learning and understanding • Now what can the students do with the information that will help them know it?
What else?	Apply Phase	• What else can students do with the information and skills? • What else is related to what students are learning or experiencing in their daily lives? • What else is done with this knowledge that the student can try?

Figure 6.1

Natural Learning Progression

Identify past, related student experiences and their impact on student knowledge and perception of the topic at hand.

Provide new insights and information, complex interrelated concepts, extensive concepts, and an opportunity to understand relationships and make multiple appropriate connections.

Engage students to act on the information, to reinforce concepts through involvement in various problem-solving, to participate in complex tasks that require open-ended strategies, etc.

Consider various ways the concepts, information, and skills can be applied in settings that are new and dynamic.

Figure 6.2

In the *process* phase, the gathered information is analyzed, compared, prioritized, and categorized in ways that make sense for the student. It is in this phase that students begin to internalize the material of the curriculum unit (Bellanca and Fogarty 1991, 90).

In the *apply* phase, the internalized information is used to create a product, is built upon to figure out the next steps, is used to imagine a different outcome, and is applied to something concrete and real in the students' lives (Bellanca and Fogarty 1991, 92).

The dimensions of inquiring, gathering, processing, and applying may not flow precisely from one to the other. For example, the gathering and processing may go back and forth for awhile before actually moving on to the applying. What is crucial is for all four phases to be included, even as they spiral back on themselves, and for the lesson and unit to culminate with the student applying the knowledge gained in the other three phases in an authentic activity or experience. It is the *apply* phase that helps students discern why all the effort of learning and studying is going on. When the application phase is shortchanged or skipped altogether, motivation is squelched. The four phases work together to create informed students who can utilize the material learned.

In addition to the four phases, Figure 6.3 includes space to write in the particular lesson focus, the two or three multiple intelligences to target that day, and the specific thinking skill and specific social skill targeted that day.

Lesson Plan

Lesson Topic:
Content Area(s):

Lesson Benchmarks/Goals	Focused Multiple Intelligences	Assessment Methods

Inquire Phase _____ Minutes	**Gather Phase** _____ Minutes	**Process Phase** _____ Minutes	**Apply Phase** _____ Minutes
Attend:	Attend:	Attend:	Attend:
Experience:	Experience:	Experience:	Experience:
Reflect:	Reflect:	Reflect:	Reflect:

Wrap-Up

Figure 6.3

The last line is for the lesson wrap-up, which could simply be concluding remarks by the teacher such as "Tomorrow we'll explore how the information you gathered today has implications for playing sports." Or, "As you can see, the insights we reflected on today reveal that the character in this play is very much like some of your friends."

Each phase is described below in terms of

- The relative potential student benefits
- The teacher's role
- Brain-compatibility

(See Figure 6.4)

The Inquire Phase

Brain research suggests students must bring previously formed patterns from long-term memory to working memory so the brain can connect new information with stored schemas as well as modify and expand them.

In the Inquire Phase Students Benefit from

- Constructing meaning of lesson content from their past experiences and stored information, knowledge, and understanding
- Identifying what they know about the lesson content, what they want to know about the subject, and eventually what they actually learned
- Participating in "communities of practice"—the learning theory that states that everyone learns as part of a group, that the collective knowledge of the group elevates each member's understanding and learning—to identify the collective knowledge, skills, and expertise of the learning group through discussions and sharing
- Demonstrating or sharing what they know or think they know about the lesson content so the teacher can identify strengths and weaknesses of the group and adjust activities and time accordingly
- Gauging their level of motivation and emotional involvement in the lesson content

The Teacher's Role in the Inquire Phase: Consultant

The role of the teacher varies within each phase and among the phases. There isn't one role that fits with each phase perfectly. All four roles can be used

Four Phases for Lesson and Unit Planning

	Inquiring	**Gathering**	**Processing**	**Applying**
Function	• Raises questions the unit will answer • Discovers prior knowledge	• Information is presented • Data and concepts are amassed • Material is observed and described	• Gathered information is analyzed, compared, prioritized and categorized	• Now understood information is used to create a product or applied to something concrete in the student's life
Student Benefit(s)	• Teacher checks what they want to get out of the lesson • Student's own knowledge is affirmed	• The students collect information by various means that accomodate each student's unique multiple intelligences	• Organizing, classifying, and categorizing new information and concepts • Making connections with prior material and experiences	• Explores ways to apply the data & concepts in ways that connect with the student's real life
Teacher's Role	• Teachers assess what the students know • Teachers assess the content and skills the students need to grasp	• Prepare mini-lectures • Model learning and thinking strategies • Invite experts • Develop learning opportunities	• Organizes individual and group activities to help construct the meaning of the information	• Enables the students to express their knowledge in various ways • Catalyzes applications beyond those in one content area
Brain Compatibility	• Draws on what the students know and have experienced • Calls upon the emotions to generate involvement	• Requires the students to become immersed in data gathering • Offers interaction with peers	• Asks students to create the meaning and significance • Students teach each other and help to clarify the data	• Encourages transfer and application of material learned • Occasions reflecting on the learning process

Figure 6.4

during each phase or combined in a variety of configurations for each phase. Teachers can select the roles they feel are most appropriate for the learning experience of students. Descriptions of the teacher's role in each phase are generalizations.

The teacher acts as a consultant by assessing what the students know, what they misunderstand, what they have experienced, and what they need to improve their understanding and develop appropriate skills.

Brain-Compatibility in the Inquire Phase

The activities in this phase are brain compatible because they
- Draw on what the students know and have experienced
- Call upon the emotions that are linked with the knowledge
- Elicit input from peers and cooperative groups
- Help students assess themselves and others
- Begin the connection-making process with new information and skills
- Do not require a prescribed set of responses or outcomes

The Gather Phase

In the gather phase students benefit from
- Thinking through concepts to arrive at an understanding that they construct instead of being supplied information without having to think about the basis or genesis of the information
- Beginning to connect new ideas and understandings to those they previously learned
- Beginning to organize, classifying, and categorizing new information and concepts
- Beginning to identify patterns and relationships among new concepts and skills
- Participating in group investigations
- Collecting information by various means that accommodate each student's unique learning style and multiple intelligences

The Teacher's Role in the Gather Phase: Presenter

As a presenter, the teacher can prepare mini-lectures, model recommended learning and thinking strategies and behaviors, present students with experiences that can teach or reinforce content, require students to present their data and/or their processes, invite experts to share their insights, and develop opportunities for students to learn from a variety of sources, including technology, resource materials like books, magazines, television, the Internet, and their peers, and any other appropriate sources.

Brain-Compatibility in the Gather Phase

The activities in this phase are brain compatible because they

- Require students to become immersed in information gathering or data collecting
- Ask students to think through the information to identify processes and to make meaning
- Offer students an opportunity to interact regularly with peers, teachers, and others who can answer questions, share information, and reinforce understanding
- Allow students a chance to learn in their preferred way without prescribing one technique or strategy
- Assist students in looking for patterns and recognizing appropriate examples
- Do not require a prescribed set of procedures for making sense of the information, so students can start with wholes and look for parts or study parts to construct wholes.

The Process Phase

In the process phase students benefit from

- Rehearsing skills in a context that is familiar and relevant
- Exploring concepts through a variety of processes, with a particular focus on the multiple intelligences
- Practicing concepts in new and challenging ways that may differ from earlier models
- Observing others as they practice to develop competencies and compare their own processes with those of others
- Receiving immediate and appropriate feedback
- Engaging in a variety of different ways of teaching and helping others understand and learn

The Teacher's Role in the Process Phase: Facilitator

The facilitator's role is to guide learning and to help students acquire knowledge and skills. The facilitator utilizes the constructivist approach to learning by designing cooperative learning activities, group discussions, and individual reflection time. The constructivist model of learning relies on the group, the group process, and individual involvement for constructing meaning from experiences and prior knowledge. The facilitator

- Organizes group activities where the synergy of group interaction discovers and constructs meaning and learning from experiences
- Leads processing and open discussions with the group(s) as they explore their understandings from experiences
- Asks participants to personally reflect on each experience

Brain-Compatibility in the Process Phase

The activities in this phase are brain compatible because they

- Require students to challenge themselves
- Ask students to think through the information again and again
- Offer students an opportunity to teach others, to clarify both understandings and misunderstandings
- Allow students a chance to learn in their preferred way without prescribing one technique or strategy
- Assist students in giving and receiving feedback
- Allow students to deviate from a prescribed set of procedures to follow the process where it takes them

The Apply Phase
In the Apply Phase Students Benefit from

- Looking for other curricular connections with the skills, knowledge, and concepts they learned
- Exploring ways to apply the lesson material that are different from what was used in the lesson
- Choosing various ways to express their understanding or demonstrate individual competence
- Evaluating the effectiveness of the learning and the validity of the information or skills they have acquired

- Taking the homework assignments and looking for ways to scaffold the learning
- Engaging others to explore and compare their understanding

The Teacher's Role in the Apply Phase: Mediator

The mediator's role is to guide, realign, and focus students' thinking and attention through learning experiences. The mediator uses metacognition activities, diagnostic/prescriptive assessments, and techniques that occasion transfer. The mediator

- Guides the direction of the reflective or introspective thinking of students
- Identifies problems or concerns of students, helps them realize their particular challenges, and assists and encourages them to modify their understandings and behaviors
- Focuses students' attention on key ideas, main themes, or critical issues. They do this by eliminating distracters such as side issues or extraneous information
- Explores with students the personal meaning and the various applications of each experience or episode.
- Encourages students to transfer their new knowledge to broader applications

When fulfilling the role of mediator, teachers need to

- Label and draw attention to their instructional strategies and behaviors
- Think "out loud" as they perform cognitive functions like problem-solving, making conceptual or informational connections, recognizing patterns, or identifying relationships
- Discuss how their experiences lead to new understandings or insights and that they occurred through self reflection, introspection, and personal evaluation
- Provide feedback to the group
- Reveal their own strengths and challenges
- Explore other applications of what has been learned by teaching students how to transfer their understanding to related disciplines and concepts
- Encourage students to do the same things modeled by the teacher

Whichever role teachers assume throughout the course of a lesson, they select the teaching strategies that will help them accomplish the role and facilitate student learning. Appropriate instructional strategies keep students focused and engaged in making meaning of the learning experiences.

Brain-Compatibility in the Apply Phase

The activities in this phase are brain compatible because they

- Require students to look for ways the information, concepts, and/or skills can be transferred to activities outside the classroom
- Ask students to search for curriculum connections, allowing the brain to make numerous links
- Offer students an opportunity to scaffold learning by engaging in homework activities that require them to extend concepts or create guidelines
- Allow students a chance to demonstrate, in a variety of ways, their understanding of the lesson content
- Assist students in reflecting on their own learning processes
- Allow students to become independent in designing additional learning activities

Attend—Experience—Reflect

Three components, attend, experience, and reflect, are central to each of the four phases and are discussed below. When beginning to design a lesson plan teachers may consult Figure 6.5 "Ways to Experience Learning," which shows where within the four-phase lesson (and where within each phase's attend-experience-reflect circuit) each activity can most effectively be used.

Attend

In the attend component teachers help students understand and appreciate what they are learning and experiencing by guiding them through each learning activity. Students learn how to think about information, how to filter out unimportant or irrelevant details, how to organize their thoughts, how to make sense of new experiences, and how to connect new information with what they already know or understand. Teachers help students focus their

Ways to Experience Learning				
	Inquire	**Gather**	**Process**	**Apply**
Analyzing			A, E, R	
Assessing		E, R		
Clarifying	A, E			
Classifying		R	E, R	
Comparing			R	A, E, R
Composing				E
Critiquing			E, R	
Diagramming		R	E, R	
Dialoguing	A, E,R	A, E, R	A, E, R	A, E, R
Discovering			E	
Dramatizing				E
Evaluate		R, E		
Exploring		E		
Graphing		R	E	
Identifying	A, E			E
Labeling	A, E			
Listing	A, E			
Logging		E		
Observing	A, E, R	E		
Painting				E
Paraphrasing			R	E
Questioning	E			
Ranking			E	
Reading		A, E		
Reflecting	R	R	R	R
Relating				
Reporting			R	E
Self-Assessing	A, R	A, R	A, R	A, R
Studying		A, E, R		
Surveying				E
Telling/Retelling				E, R
Uncovering	E			

Figure 6.5

A = during the ATTEND part of the activity
E = during the EXPERIENCE part of the activity
R = during the REFLECT part of the activity

SkyLight Professional Development

concentration and raise their level of consciousness or mindfulness by asking discerning questions and by assigning students specific cognitive tasks.

The purpose of the attend section within each phase is for students to begin to make meaning of each learning experience or new information. During every experience students should focus on the meaning of the experience by reflecting on or thinking about particular aspects of the experience as they occur. Thinking during the experience is as important as the experience itself. And helping students filter out extraneous information or helping them focus their attention is itself an important learning process.

Experience

Learning is ultimately active and experiential; therefore, the learning activities, instructional strategies, and experiences presented to students in the experience section will affect students' perception, thought processes, and ability to process the activity's content.

Reflect

Reflection, as used here, is a thinking process in which teachers lead students through intrapersonal reflections and group discussions to assist students in a meaning-making process. Reflecting on a learning experience requires students to revisit the thinking they were encouraged to attend to throughout the learning activity. Reflection gives students a chance to process and discuss what they have just learned or experienced. As students encounter new information, they need time to make sense of it and to connect what they have learned with other things they already know or understand. When students share their perceptions and understandings, they offer insights to each other. Such social interaction reinforces what the students learned or challenges what they think they learned. As students verbalize or write down what they understand, they are forming an observable expression of their comprehension for themselves, their classmates, and/or the teacher depending upon the reflection activity. They are able to consider again and again what they just experienced. Revisiting the learning activity assists students in creating meaning from the information and consequently strengthening brain connections with prior knowledge and experience.

As students share their perceptions, understandings, and insights, they reinforce learning or challenge the thinking. As students express what they think they understand, they are required to express their comprehension of the material and to consider again and again what they just experienced. Revisiting the learning activity assists students in formulating the meaning of the information and in strengthening connections with patterns they have already established.

Internal Structure

Inherent in the four phases is the idea that at least four different activities are included in each lesson. However, teachers may include additional activities in selected phases, or even revisit that phase at a later time in the lesson, depending on the desired emphasis or the needs of the students. By engaging in at least four different activities students

- Participate in four Beginning-End-Middle (BEM) cycles
- Cycle through at least four attend-experience-reflect sequences
- Benefit from pulsed learning
- Interact with the information in four different ways, allowing different learning styles and intelligences to be used
- Stay on task within the recommended "age plus or minus two minutes" time frame
- Receive feedback at least four different times from the teacher, from peers, or through self-evaluation
- Take time to build understanding through the use of multiple examples or experiences
- Engage in metacognition and processing of the lesson at least four times throughout the lesson

Integrated Assessment

The attend and reflect sections of the attend-experience-reflect sequence of each phase of the lesson plan are ideal for integrating assessment and learning. (See sample lessons at the end of chapters 1 through 5.) During the attend activities, students can focus on the requirements of a job well done illustrated by a criterion-based rubric. Keeping the requirements in mind as a standard, students can monitor themselves during each learning experience. The reflect strategies can serve as the checkpoint for students to reflect on how their performance compares with the rubric. The continual evaluation helps students determine how closely their behavior approximates the ideal standard. The extended-time format provides teachers with the opportunity to engage regularly in the attend and reflect activities critical for integrating authentic assessment tools into a teaching design.

Unit Design

A unit is a division of information for study supported by state and/or national benchmarks and standards. (See chapter 3 for a discussion of the development and impact of standards on curriculum.) Standards that are knowledge related, that support understanding of major concepts, and that provide required skill development form the underpinnings for the teaching unit. Units can be centered around

- Themes (human rights or life)
- Concepts (gravity or democracy)
- Issues (women's suffrage or religious differences that lead to political and social crises)
- Skills (short story writing or the use of a protractor or other measurement device)
- Problems to solve (any shortage or scarcity or pollution)
- Knowledge to relate (historical events and their contemporary counterparts)

Units follow a developmental process to ensure the acquisition of both skills and understanding. Figure 6.6 provides an outline for teachers to construct four-phase unit plans of their own. In addition to the four phases, the blank "Unit Plan" page includes space to note the unit standards and curriculum goals, the particular multiple intelligences to be stressed overall, and the assessment tools and methods for the unit. The wrap-up could include remarks by the teacher concerning how the unit will connect to the next one; a mention of how this unit has implications for other content disciplines; or a comment on what he or she is particularly pleased with in terms of the class work on the unit.

The Lesson/Unit Dynamic

Units need to be composed of an adequate number of lessons to ensure that objectives of the unit are met. The unit follows the same cycle as the lesson

Unit Plan

Unit Topic:

Content Area:

Unit Content Standards/Goals	Focused Multiple Intelligences	Assessment Methods

Inquire Phase ____ Class Meetings	**Gather Phase** ____ Class Meetings	**Process Phase** ____ Class Meetings	**Apply Phase** ____ Class Meetings

Wrap-Up

Figure 6.6

Emphasis at Each Phase of the Unit				
Inquire Phase			Gather Phase	Process Phase	Apply Phase
Inquire Phase	Gather Phase		Process Phase	Apply Phase
Inquire Phase	Gather Phase	Process Phase		Apply Phase
Inquire Phase	Gather Phase	Process Phase	Apply Phase	

Figure 6.7

(inquire-gather-process-apply). It is important to remember that while each lesson within the unit has four phases the lessons themselves may be concentrated in one phase more than the others. Figure 6.7 "Emphasis at Each Phase of the Unit" illustrates the lesson emphasis at each phase of the unit.

In addition, enough time needs to be allocated for student understanding and skill acquisition and for student demonstration of understanding and skills. Units may last for one week or for three to four weeks. The number of lessons could then range from five lessons in a one-week unit up to twenty lessons in a four-week unit on a 4 by 4 Block schedule. In a Block 8 schedule, the number of lessons stays the same, but the weeks to cover the units are doubled.

The school year can be separated into the following timeframes:

36 weeks = Year-long course; from 12 to 18 units

18 weeks = Semester or $1/2$-year course; from 6 to 9 units

12 weeks = Trimester or $1/3$-year course; from 3 to 6 units

3 week = mini-course; 1 or 2 units

If a month-long unit in traditional schedules has now become just two weeks in a 4 by 4, for example, these four phases can be laid out over the two weeks.

Day One: The Inquiry Phase

Days Two through Five: The Gather Phase, pulling together all the necessary information on the unit at hand

Days Six through Eight: The Process Phase, spent using various methods and working with the material gathered in the previous phase

Days Nine and Ten: The Apply Phase, in which the material is applied, expanded on, or something new is created from it.

Such a plan calls for a whole new form of information delivery. It absolutely necessitates using the students to prepare and deliver some of that information and demands the teacher become a facilitator in addition to being the instructor.

The four-phase unit format that encourages meaning making for each successive experience throughout the unit mirrors the cycle followed in lesson design. Each lesson of the unit is an experience, and the progression of experiences throughout the unit helps students in their individual meaning making of the unit goals and objectives.

The unit format, the lesson design, and the teaching strategies used throughout the unit are based on brain research and proven instructional techniques for facilitating learning. There are four fundamental strategies that serve as the basis for each unit of instruction: cooperative learning, multiple intelligences, higher-order thinking skills, and graphic organizers. (See chapter 4 for a discussion of each.)

Before designing the content flow and sequence of the unit, teachers can ask themselves these essential questions:

- What are the key concepts students need to learn during this unit?
- What skills ("know how") do the students need to demonstrate and represent their understanding of the concepts?
- What are some individual and general applications ("know why") of the key concepts?
- What experiences will provide students with not only emotional connections to the concepts but also the invaluable insights into the meaning and applications of the concepts?

After the framework for the unit has been set (see Figure 6.8), the teacher then determines the delivery structure. In the case of the biology unit example, thematic instruction is used in the inquire phase, problem-based instruction and case studies in the gather phase, performance learning in the process phase, and both project and service learning in the apply phase. The lessons are then "hung from" the scaffold of the delivery structure.

INQUIRE PHASE

The purpose of the first phase of the unit is to investigate what students know about the unit concepts and what skills they possess and to identify the goals and objectives of the unit. In addition, during the first phase the teacher along with students may decide how to assess changes in student "know how" and "know why."

Unit Plan

Unit Topic: *Cardiovascular system*
Content Area: *Biology*

Unit Content Standards/Goals	Focused Multiple Intelligences	Assessment Methods
Understands the major systems of the human body	*Logical/Mathematical* *Bodily/Kinesthetic* *Visual/Spatial* *Verbal/Linguistic*	*Project rubric* *Quiz* *Self-evaluation* *Peer performance evaluation*

Inquire Phase __*I*__ Class Meeting(s)	**Gather Phase** __*3*__ Class Meeting(s)	**Process Phase** __*2*__ Class Meeting(s)	**Apply Phase** __*2*__ Class Meeting(s)
Video excerpt "Incredible Journey" *Discussion* *Web graphic organizer on definition of systems* *Small group study of paragraphs on social, biological, ecological, and solar systems* *Fishbone graphic organizer on traits of systems* *KWL on cardiovascular system*	*Describe projects* • *design a video presentation for PBS on how to keep your CV system healthy* • *sculpt a detailed model of the CV system* • *create a brochure containing guideliines for person recovering from heart attacks* *Create project plans* *Share info sources* *Submit project plan*	*Each team creates a matrix, fishbone, or concept web on info gathered* *Debate:* • *Exercise has/has no effect* • *Tension has/has no effect* • *Unhealthy diet has/has no effect* *Quiz on important facts and details* *Give time to work on projects*	*Finish projects* *Present projects* *Self-evaluation in journal* *Peer performance evaluation checklist*

Wrap-Up
Show how this unit provides a bridge between what was studied up until now and future work.

Figure 6.8

GATHER PHASE

The goal of the gather phase of the unit is to obtain information that introduces students to new ideas, concepts, or skills. Teachers can also select activities that help students understand why they each have diverse associations or different understandings regarding the new information and skills. Students can also be assisted in linking the new information with their past experiences and connecting their new knowledge with insights and concepts they have stored in long-term memory. During this phase, teachers can select examples that place the new information and skills into context for the students. Context provides students with an understanding of how useful and practical the new information and skills can be.

PROCESS PHASE

Processing the new knowledge and skills that students have acquired during the gather phase occurs through a variety of activities. Students can participate in practice drills, in peer tutoring, in preparing charts and graphs, or in any number of student performances that will reinforce their understandings, clarify any misunderstandings they might have, and possibly add new understandings or insights related to the unit concepts.

APPLY PHASE

During this last phase of the unit, the focus of the learning activities is on relating the new knowledge and skills to real-life settings. Relevance and application are the primary goals of this phase. In order for students to transfer unit concepts to other courses they are taking and to other real-life experiences, students can be asked to look for examples of who, how, and when they have seen others use the skills and knowledge presented during the unit. They can be asked to make connections to activities with which they are already engaged. Further, they can share with each other the insights they have gained as they have reflected on the unit concepts and how they can be applied to their lives.

Function Follows Form

The four-phase plan presented here is important for teachers to follow because it reminds them of the various components of the learning process and of the reason for using the strategies they use. It can help them provide diversity in learning opportunities for students. The design can help teachers remember to include successful strategies and techniques they used to use but discarded, lost, or forgot over time. In addition, it helps teachers think about and evaluate the effectiveness of their instructional strategies. The lesson design also helps students recognize a process they can use when designing their own learning experiences.

APPENDIX 1
USING INTERNET RESOURCES TO ENERGIZE LEARNING IN THE BLOCK

Finding Web Sites

Search engines, such as Alta Vista, Yahoo!, and Snap, search the immensity of information on the World Wide Web and report back a number of sites potential relevant to the search term the user inputs. A recent search of the term "block scheduling" resulted in 18,013, matches and one for the term "brain-compatible learning" yielded 57,924! Obviously, it is impractical to investigate each of the sites found. Fortunately, software programs (such as Web Compass) offer Internet search tools that locate, categorize, and summarize Web sites according to the user's specifications. In addition, books such as *1001 of the Best Internet Sites for Educators* by Mark Treadwell (1999) can save educators precious time and trouble surfing for sites.

Evaluating Web Sites

Associations including the American Association of School Libraries (www.ala.org/ICONN/curricu2.html) and the Mid-Continent Regional Educational Laboratory, or McREL (www.mcrel.org/connect/plus/critical.html) offer criteria for evaluating the usefulness of Internet sites.

The most desirable sites for education purposes possess the following characteristics:
- Download quickly
- Contain accurate, bias-free information
- Provide functioning links to other pertinent sites
- Display as few advertising messages and/or solicitations as possible

Useful Content Sites for the Sample Four-Phase Lesson Plans

The sites' URLs (Uniform Resource Locators) appear for each as the Internet address. The Web protocol for each site is http://. In addition to domain names (as in www.skylightedu.com), subdirectory information is provided so that the user can obtain specific data. Information stored at a site's subdirectory is separated from the domain name by a slash (as is the case with www.skylightedu.com/teachered). Each site below was functioning at the stated URL as this book went to press.

Sample Four-Phase Lesson Plan #1: *What's on Your Mind*
The Neuroscience on the Web Series
www.csuchico.edu/~pmccaff/syllabi/spp/365/index.html

Dr. Koop.com
www.drkoop.com/Depression
For the mental health section (adolescent depression, eating and anxiety disorders, and suicide prevention)

Sample Four-Phase Lesson Plan # 2: *Can Prejudice Kill a Mockingbird?*
To Kill a Mockingbird & Harper Lee
www.chebucto.ns.ca/culture/HarperLee/index.html

Sample Four-Phase Lesson Plan # 4: *Gender, Age, and Pyramids*
The National Geographic's Map Machine
www.nationalgeographic.com/maps/atlas/index.html

A Note About Web Safety

Many schools plugged into the Internet use some type of *censorware,* a type of software program used to filter out inappropriate or objectionable material. However, these programs are not infallible. Educators using Internet sites as part of lessons or assignments need to monitor and direct student "visits" into cyberspace. One way to keep students away from objectionable, or even time-wasting, sites is to bookmark the sites the teacher has visited and found to be valuable to the lesson at hand.

APPENDIX 2
BLANK LESSON PLAN

Unit #:
Chapter #:
Lesson #:   Time: X minutes

Competency:
National Standards:

Lesson Question:

SCANS
Fundamental Skills

- [ ] Basic Skills
- [ ] Thinking Skills
- [ ] Personal Qualities

Workplace Competencies

- [ ] Resources
- [ ] Interpersonal
- [ ] Information
- [ ] Systems
- [ ] Technology

Multiple Intelligences

- [ ] Bodily/Kinesthetic
- [ ] Visual/Spatial
- [ ] Logical/ Mathematical
- [ ] Verbal/Linguistic
- [ ] Musical/ Rhythmical
- [ ] Naturalist
- [ ] Interpersonal
- [ ] Intrapersonal

Thinking Skills
Sternberg's P-A-C

- [ ] Practical
- [ ] Analytical
- [ ] Creative

Bloom's Taxonomy

- [ ] Knowledge
- [ ] Comprehension
- [ ] Application
- [ ] Analysis
- [ ] Synthesis
- [ ] Evaluation

Structured Reflection

- [ ] Metacognition
- [ ] What?
    So What?
    Now What?
- [ ] Socratic Dialog
- [ ] E-I-A-G

Graphic Organizers

- [ ] Mind Map
- [ ] Concept Web
- [ ] Sunshine Wheel
- [ ] Fishbone
- [ ] Matrix
- [ ] KWL
- [ ] Venn Diagram
- [ ] Sequence
- [ ] T-Chart
- [ ] Double T-Chart
- [ ] P-M-I
- [ ] Other

Authentic Assessment

- [ ] Observation Checklist
- [ ] Portfolio
- [ ] Rubric
- [ ] Test and Quizzes
- [ ] Graphic Organizers
- [ ] Notebook Entries
- [ ] Logs
- [ ] Performance
- [ ] Project

Lesson Objectives

Legend:
- [ ] Indicates item is not used in lesson
- [ ] Indicates item is used in lesson

Materials and Key Words:

Supplies:

Resources:

High End Option:

Low End Option:

Key Words: (Found in student textbook)

Setup:

Energizer—

Inquire—

Gather—

Process—

Apply—

Lesson Preview:

Inquire:

Gather:

Process:

Apply:

Assessment:

Lesson Plan

Icebreaker/Energizer:

Supplies:

Resources:

Setup:

Direct Cadet Focus: (Time: X minutes)

Learning Activity: (Time: X minutes)

Reflection: (Time: X minutes)

Total Time: X minutes

Phase I—Inquire:
Supplies:
Resources:
Setup:

Direct Cadet Focus: (Time: X minutes)

Learning Activity: (Time: X minutes)

Reflection: (Time: X minutes)

Total Time: X minutes

Phase 2—Gather:

Supplies:

Resources:

Setup:

Direct Cadet Focus: (Time: X minutes)

Learning Activity: (Time: X minutes)

Reflection: (Time: X minutes)

Total Time: X minutes

Phase 3—Process:
Supplies:
Resources:
Setup:

Direct Cadet Focus: (Time: X minutes)

Learning Activity: (Time: X minutes)

Reflection: (Time: X minutes)

Total Time: X minutes

Phase 4—Apply:
Supplies:
Resources:

Setup:

Direct Cadet Focus: (Time: X minutes)

Learning Activity: (Time: X minutes)

Reflection: (Time: X minutes)

Homework:

Assessment:

Total Time: X minutes

APPENDIX 3
SAMPLE LESSON PLAN

Unit 3: *Foundations for Success*
Chapter 1: *Know Yourself—Socrates*
Lesson 1: *Self Awareness*   Time: 90 minutes

Competency: *Develop self-understanding and an appreciation for diversity.*
National Standards: *NL-ENG.K–12.3 Evaluation Strategies, NL-ENG.K–12.4 Communication Skills,*
NL-ENG.K–12.11 Participating In Society, NL-ENG.K–12.12 Applying Language Skills
Lesson Question: *How are behaviors categorized using Winning Colors®?*

SCANS
Fundamental Skills
- ☒ Basic Skills
- ☒ Thinking Skills
- ☒ Personal Qualities

Workplace Competencies
- ☐ Resources
- ☒ Interpersonal
- ☒ Information
- ☐ Systems
- ☐ Technology

Multiple Intelligences
- ☒ Bodily/Kinesthetic
- ☒ Visual/Spatial
- ☐ Logical/Mathematical
- ☒ Verbal/Linguistic
- ☒ Musical/Rhythmical
- ☐ Naturalist
- ☒ Interpersonal
- ☒ Intrapersonal

Thinking Skills Sternberg's P-A-C
- ☐ Practical
- ☒ Analytical
- ☒ Creative

Bloom's Taxonomy
- ☒ Knowledge
- ☒ Comprehension
- ☒ Application
- ☒ Analysis
- ☒ Synthesis
- ☐ Evaluation

Structured Reflection
- ☒ Metacognition
- ☒ What?
   So What?
   Now What?
- ☐ Socratic Dialog
- ☐ E-I-A-G

Graphic Organizers
- ☐ Mind Map
- ☐ Concept Web
- ☐ Sunshine Wheel
- ☐ Fishbone
- ☒ Matrix
- ☐ KWL
- ☐ Venn Diagram
- ☐ Sequence
- ☐ T-Chart
- ☒ Double T-Chart
- ☐ P-M-I
- ☐ Other

Authentic Assessment
- ☒ Observation Checklist
- ☐ Portfolio
- ☐ Rubric
- ☐ Test and Quizzes
- ☐ Graphic Organizers
- ☒ Notebook Entries
- ☐ Logs
- ☐ Performance
- ☐ Project

Lesson Objectives
Using the Winning Colors, framework, explain four clusters of behavior in positive terms.

Illustrate your present behavioral preferences by arranging the four Winning Colors, cards as directed.

Use an example of what you did in a specific situation to explain the card arrangement.

Identify the strength of each behavior cluster, for you personally, by arranging the cards as directed.

Demonstrate self-esteem in your attitude and communication practices by expressing appreciation for your own uniqueness.

Legend:
- ☐ Indicates item is not used in lesson
- ☒ Indicates item is used in lesson

Materials and Key Words:

Supplies: *Chart paper, Colored markers (brown, blue, green, red), Colored pencils or crayons, Index cards, Large paper, Magazines, Mirror, Glue, Scissors, Small pieces of paper or sticky notes, Tape*

Resources: *Key Words, Objectives, Assessment 1, Audio 1, Exercise 1–2, Koosh ball, Notebooks, Student text, Emotional Intelligence Programs CD-ROM, Videos 1–2, Winning Colors® (WC) cards*

High End Option: *Unit 3 CD-ROM, Computer, Monitor*

Low End Option: *Overhead projector, CD/Tape player, Classical music, TV/VCR, "Winning Colors" videotape*

Key Words: *(Found in student textbook) Assessment, Associate, Cluster, Differentiate, Introspection*

Setup:

Energizer—*Option 1: Play Video 1. Provide large paper and art supplies. Option 2: Play Audio 1.*

Inquire—*Display key words and objectives. Display questions. Distribute small pieces of paper or sticky notes to cadets.*

Gather—*Copy and distribute Exercise 1. Option 1: Distribute WC cards. Prepare to play Video 2 or "Winning Colors" videotape. Option 2: Setup TV/VCR.*

Process—*Draw and label Matrix, by color/behavior, on the board or chart paper.*

Apply—*Play Audio 1. Copy and distribute Exercise 2.*

Lesson Preview:

Note: You may decide to teach this lesson using the Emotional Intelligence Workshop located on the Emotional Intelligence Programs CD-ROM. To access the program and recommended resources, please refer to the CD's Quick Start Manual. It gives cadets the background on emotional intelligence, why it is important, and introduces the Personal Skills Map and Winning Colors self-assessments.

Inquire:

Option 1: Teams perform a carousel, brainstorming activity to come up with a team answer for each question about them.

Option 2: Cadets brainstorm in small teams to come up with several answers that explore what they know about themselves.

Option 3: Cadets provide several answers that explore what they know about themselves individually, then read and discuss each other's answers anonymously.

Self-paced Option: Cadets write out three or four examples to answer each question.

Gather:

Option 1: Provide structure and a framework for understanding by presenting behavior clusters, using Winning Colors (WC). Show video clip and use mini-lecture to present WC to the cadets. Cadets use Exercise 1 to self-assess color dominance.

Option 2: Cadets watch "Winning Colors" videotape and assess communication powers.

Self-paced Option: Cadets read the student text to learn about WC communication powers, complete Exercise 1: Discover your Communication Power and record their results.

Process:

One team role-plays a scenario to bring out many behavioral preferences, while remaining cadets observe and take note.

Self-paced Option: Cadets identify someone famous (dead or alive) who is a planner, adventurer, builder, or relater and write a notebook entry explaining their classification.

Apply:

Cadets reflect on what they have learned about themselves and to capture that data in Exercise 2: Self Awareness Matrix.

Self-paced Option: Same as above.

Assessment:

Use Assessment 1: Matrix Checklist.

Lesson Plan

Icebreaker/Energizer:

Supplies: *Colored pencils or crayons, Large paper*

Resources: *CD/Tape player, Audio 1: Classical Music, Mirror, Video 1: Self-Portraits Animation, Tape, Unit 3 CD-ROM, Computer, Monitor, or Overhead projector*

Setup:
Option 1:
1. Play Video 1: Self-Portraits Animation from Unit 3 CD-ROM.
2. Provide large sheets of paper and art supplies (colored pencils or crayons) to cadets.

Option 2:
Play Audio 1: Classical Music from Unit 3 CD-ROM or CD/Tape player.

Direct Cadet Focus: (Time: 1 minute)
Tell cadets:
- *Artists, who create self-portraits, depict in their drawings a sense of their unique characteristics, persona, interests and way of life.*
- *Think about what your self-portrait would be like, if you could paint your own self-image.*
- *Focus on whether you see yourself the same way others might see you.*

Learning Activity: (Time: 7 minutes)
Option 1:
1. *During the Self-portraits animation, ask cadets:*
   - *What is the artist doing or communicating about him or herself in this portrait?*
   - *How do you see yourself versus what others see in you?*
   - *When you look in the mirror, what do you see?*
   Note: Provide mirror for cadets who want to look at themselves for this reason.
2. *Direct cadets to sketch a quick self-portrait of themselves using the supplied materials.*
3. *Remind cadets to include something in their picture that will tell others about who they are, what they like to do, where they live, etc.*
4. *Cadets may sign their names and tape their drawings on the wall, or they may wish to complete them as homework.*

Option 2:
1. *Form teams of 2–5 cadets.*
2. *Direct cadets to introduce themselves in the third person, to their team members, as if introducing their best friend.*
   Note: Supply questions to answer here so the introductions elicit the kind of information wanted for the Inquire phase. Sample questions/categories: "In your introduction, tell us (1) one fun activity to do with this person, (2) what they like about working in a team, or (3) one or two words that describe them.

Reflection: (Time: 2 minutes)
Ask cadets the following questions:
- *What you have just learned about yourself?*
- *What you have just learned about your classmates?*
- *Why is it important to know yourself and what you stand for?*
- *Does the fact that everyone is unique, play into your own self-image?*

Total Time: 10 minutes

Phase I—Inquire:

Supplies: *Chart paper, Colored markers, Small pieces of paper or sticky notes, Tape*

Resources: *Key words, Objectives, Unit 3 CD-ROM, Computer, Monitor, or Overhead projector*

Setup:

1. *Display objectives and key words on board or from Unit 3 CD-ROM.*
2. *Distribute small pieces of paper or sticky notes to cadets.*
3. *On the board, create and display a Double T-Chart with one of the following questions on each column:*
   - *How do you interact with others socially, to enjoy yourself?*
   - *How do you complete individual tasks or assignments?*
   - *How you deal with other people in a team or committee that has a job requiring teamwork?*

   Note: Instead of using the board, you may display each question on separate pieces of chart paper and post them at stations around the room.

Direct Cadet Focus: (Time: 2 minutes)

1. *Ask cadets to think about each of the displayed questions.*
2. *Read the question aloud, and then provide an example from your own life to answer each question. This will give cadets an idea of what you are looking for.*
3. *Tell cadets that they will be brainstorming to answer the questions; there are no right or wrong behavior descriptions, nor does a behavior have to be something done all the time. The goal is to get a lot of information quickly.*

Learning Activity: (Time: 14 minutes)

Note: Post all examples. This is a brainstorming activity; if they say it, it goes up without censure or judgment (unless inappropriate). However, do not post cadet names next to examples.

Option 1:

1. *Form teams of 2-3 cadets.*
2. *Teams talk briefly among themselves to determine answers.*
3. *Direct teams to post an example, using a descriptive word or short phrase.*

Option 2:

1. *Form teams with no more than 4 cadets each.*
2. *Have teams discuss all three questions or, to save time, assign one question per team.*
3. *During their discussion, cadets will record answers on slips of paper.*
4. *Each team will tape or write their examples under the questions.*

Option 3:

1. *Direct cadets to write out three or four examples each in answer to the questions, and post their answers under each question.*
2. *Have all the cadets go around to each chart and read all of the entries. They should find entries that are similar or different and be prepared to state why they grouped things together and what is the same or different about items in the group(s).*

Self-paced Option: Cadets write out three or four examples to answer each question.

Reflection: (Time: 4 minutes)

Ask cadets the following questions:

- *What did you notice about how people in our class deal with people in social situations?*
- *What have you learned about how different people handle assignments or tasks?*
- *What would help you improve your ability to work with others?*

Total Time: 20 minutes

Phase 2—Gather:

Supplies: *Chart paper, Colored markers (brown, blue, green, red)*

Resources: *Exercise 1: Discover your Communication Power, Notebooks, Student text, Winning Colors®
(WC) cards, Video 2: Winning Colors or "Winning Colors" videotape, Unit 3 CD-ROM, Computer, Monitor, or
TV/VCR*

Setup:

Copy and distribute Exercise 1: Discover your Communication Power.

Option 1:

1. Distribute a set of WC cards to each pair of cadets.

2. Prepare to play Video 2: Winning Colors from Unit 3 CD-ROM.

Option 2:

Setup TV/VCR to play "Winning Colors" videotape.

Direct Cadet Focus: (Time: 1 minute)

Tell cadets:

- *Think about the different behavioral clusters and try to determine which of your Winning Colors® are
  the strongest now: planner, builder, relater, or adventurer.*
- *The four parts of self and your power to communicate reside in your ability to exhibit different behaviors
  in situations. Although everyone is comprised of each of the behaviors in diverse extents, the goal of
  Winning Colors® is to work to develop a balance between the four colors.*

Learning Activity: (Time: 25 minutes)

Option 1:

1. Present a mini-lecture to introduce Winning Colors® (WC) to cadets.

*2. Use a story, parable, or familiar characters from media to give cadets vivid, familiar examples of the
   concepts you present to enhance comprehension and retention. Examples:*

- *Snow White - the Wicked Stepmother is a Planner and Snow White is a Relater. The Dwarves are
  Builders as a group but individual Relaters, Planners, and Adventurers make up the group.*
- *Star Trek, the Next Generation - Picard is a Builder and Counselor. Troy is a Planner.*
- *Behaviors identified by certain cadets during class.*

3. Cover the four behavioral clusters and make these points:

- *The Name of the Cluster*
- *The Associated Color*
- *The Associated Animal*
- *The Primary Action Word*

  *Note: Here are the points for each card: Builder (brown, bull and bear, decide); Relater (blue, dolphin,
  feel); Planner (green, fox, think); and Adventurer (red, tiger, act).*

4. Form cadets into pairs.

5. Cadets Think-Share-Pair.

- *Each cadet takes two cards, picture side up.*
- *Tell cadets to look at the picture side for a minute, then turn the cards over and read the back.*
- *Afterwards, have pairs share together what they have learned. Each person should present
  information about the two cards they studied to their partner.*

6. Play the Winning Colors® video from the Unit 3 CD-ROM.

7. Cadets sort their Winning Colors® (WC) cards to determine dominant colors. Ask cadets to:

- *Use the cards to describe their own behavior, by sorting them in the order of strongest, or most
  common, to weakest, or rarely displayed.*
- *Think about how they actually see themselves behaving, not how they behave for others or wish they
  would be, then sort the cards as they feel inside or see themselves at this time.*
- *Place the behavior cluster they display most often up at the 12 o'clock position, and then continue
  around the clock to form a circle from strongest to weakest.*
- *Enter their WC sort as a notebook entry with the date and the numbers 1-4, with 1 being the
  strongest behavior.*

Note: State that there is no right or wrong way to sort the cards and no card is better than another is. Advise them to avoid the temptation to pick the Adventurer card first because of peer pressure.

8. *Cadets complete Exercise 1: Discover your Communication Power to get a numerical value for the strength of each behavior.*

9. *When finished, each pair goes up to the questions charts from the Inquire phase and votes; that is, cadets indicate which behavior cluster they believe is represented by each example. Record votes with a colored dot next to each item: brown, blue, green, or red.*

Option 2:

Play the "Winning Colors" videotape (from the beginning until after the poetry scene) for cadets and then have them complete Exercise 1: Discover your Communication Power and record their results.

Self-paced Option:

Cadets read the student text to learn about WC communication powers, complete Exercise 1: Discover your Communication Power and record their results.

Reflection: (Time: 4 minutes)

Ask cadets the following questions:

* *Did some examples get different color votes? Why?*
* *What color dominates our charts? What does this say about our class and us as individuals?*
* *What does it say about the questions on the charts? Would the colors be different if we asked another question? How?*

Total Time: 30 minutes

Phase 3—Process:

Supplies: *Chart paper, Colored markers (brown, blue, green, red)*

Resources: *Koosh ball, Notebooks, Unit 3 CD-ROM, Computer, Monitor, or Overhead projector*

Setup:

Draw a 2-column by 2-row Matrix on the board or chart paper. Label each square with a different color/behavior. See sample below:

Green/Planner	*Blue/Relater*
Brown/Builder	*Red/Adventurer*

Direct Cadet Focus: (Time: 1 minute)

Direct cadets to reflect on what behaviors they display everyday that would let others determine your dominant behaviors. Ask cadets:

* *How could you identify what colors others exhibit on a regular basis?*
* *What color do you think is my dominate color and why?*

Learning Activity: (Time: 10 minutes)

1. *Form a team of 4 cadets (with different dominant colors) to role-play a scenario while the rest of the class observes.*

Note: For large classes, set up two teams doing the same thing, so you can bring them all back into the large team to debrief and compare notes.

2. *Read cadets the following scenario:*

   You belong to a service club and are on a team of 4 people who are organizing a Halloween party for the neighborhood children. The team's mission is to plan a fun-filled evening for the kids, you have a budget of $150, and about 20 people have volunteered to help.

3. *Direct cadets in the role-play to "let their true colors show" and act out the scenario while observers take notes on when the different behavior clusters (act, think, feel, or decide) are displayed.*

4. *Use the Koosh ball to brainstorm among cadet observers. Direct cadets with the Koosh ball to identify a specific example and the color displayed, write it in the Matrix, and toss the ball to another observer.*

Self-paced Option:

Notebook entry:

• *Ask cadets to identify someone famous (dead or alive) who is a planner, adventurer, builder, or relater. For example: Jim Morrison was an adventurer; Oprah Winfrey is a relater; Martha Stewart is a planner; and Alan Greenspan is a builder.*

• *Cadets write a notebook entry to suggest why that person exhibits the behavior cluster identified.*

Reflection: (Time: 4 minutes)

Ask cadets the following questions:

• *Did you see people get in a behavior preference and stay there, or move between several?*

• *What do you think you would have done for the carnival committee?*

• *What does that say about your behavior preferences?*

Total Time: 15 minutes

Phase 4—Apply:

Supplies: *Chart paper, Markers*

Resources: *Assessment 1: Matrix Checklist, CD/Tape player, Audio 1: Classical Music, Exercise 2: Self Awareness Matrix, Notebooks, Unit 3 CD-ROM, Computer, Monitor, or Overhead projector*

Setup:

1. *Play Audio 1: Classical Music from Unit 3 CD-ROM or CD/Tape player.*

2. *Copy and distribute Exercise 2: Self Awareness Matrix.*

Direct Cadet Focus: (Time: 1 minute)

Remind cadets that their Winning Colors® are behaviors they have now and those they should develop; they can view the behavior of others with the understanding that all people have behavioral preferences and strengths.

Learning Activity: (Time: 10 minutes)

1. *Ask cadets to spend the next few minutes thinking of situations in their lives. Ask them to think of situations with these dynamics:*

   • *A new relationship is starting up.*

   • *People have a common goal.*

   • *People are in conflict.*

2. *Now ask cadets to pick one of the situations, because they care about it, it is very interesting or complicated, or for whatever reason it is important to them.*

3. *Suggest they consider the situation in the light of what they are learning about themselves. Have cadets describe the situation in notebooks or to a partner, using what they have learned about their Winning Colors®.*

4. *Direct cadets to complete Exercise 2: Self Awareness Matrix individually and turn it in to get credit.*

Note: Return exercise when marked and recommend cadets add it to their personal portfolios.

Self-paced Option: Same as above.

Reflection: (Time: 4 minutes)

Ask cadets the following questions:

• *What have you learned about yourself as a member of a team and as an individual?*

• *How about in terms of work and play?*

Homework:

Direct cadets to create a self-portrait of themselves (if they haven't done so already), or work on the details of the one started in the Icebreaker phase.

Assessment:

Use Assessment 1: Matrix Checklist.

Total Time: 15 minutes

GLOSSARY

Assessment—the process of gathering information about what students know and can do.

Benchmark—defines the prescribed quality level of student work.

Block scheduling—a time schedule that allows for extended class periods. Moving from forty or fifty minute periods to eighty or one hundred minute class periods.

Brain model (also, brain schema or mental schema)—the picture or concept the brain comes up with to make sense out of material that has been input.

Conferences—a form of gathering evidence of what a student or a group of students have learned.

Copernican plan—perhaps the most flexible and most complex of the block scheduling models; allows some courses to be taught in thirty or sixty days with very extended time formats.

Constructivist Learning Theory—the notion that learners construct their own unique concepts through active participation and meaning making.

Extrinsic motivation—motivation that is catalyzed by some external reward (money, grades, stickers, food, etc.).

Graphic organizer—simple pictures or images that serve as tools to organize information.

Intrinsic motivation—motivation that is catalyzed by some internal reward (the joy of working on something one is interested in, the satisfaction of learning something for the sake of learning something, the pleasure of learning something that one is interested in).

Log—notebook in which student reflections on content material read or studied in class can be written.

Metacognition—the act of stepping back and thinking about one's own thinking, about how one thinks; the act of reflecting on one's own thought processes; thinking about thinking.

Metacognitive journal—notebook of sorts in which one writes personal reflections on life and/or learning experiences.

Observation checklist—a list of targeted behaviors or activities that are being taught or assessed at a particular time.

Performance learning—curricular framework in which students enact or carry out a specific process or task such as a musical piece, a dance step, a scientific lab process, a speech, an individual or group presentation, a role play about a particular period in history, a dramatic re-creation of a Shakespearean play in modern times, etc.

Portfolio—a collection of student samples that reveal the learning and growth that has taken place over a period of time.

Project learning—curricular framework from which the student completes a specific objective task such as a model of an ancient Roman village, a video on an environmental project on river clean-up, a brochure about travel opportunities in the country of the foreign language being studied, etc.

Pulsed activities—alternating higher-intensity activities with lower-intensity activities to allow for processing of the material.

Rubric—a set of criteria with progressive indicators used to assess a student's performance or project. The criteria and indicators are specific enough that both the teacher and the student are crystal clear ahead of time about what is expected in the performance or project.

Selective abandonment—the setting aside of curriculum material in order to create a more workable amount of curriculum for the semester, the trimester, or the unit.

Standardized test—a test prepared by a regionally or nationally central office to determine how a student or a school is doing compared to other students or schools in the region or in the nation. Traditionally such tests have emphasized the memorization of curriculum details assessed through multiple-choice or true-false questions.

BIBLIOGRAPHY

Baylis, Clifford A. 1983. From "Summary of an investigation into the relative effects on student performance on a "block" vs. "non-block" scheduled developmental semester," a paper presented to the Developmental Education Committee at Allegheny County College, Monroeville, Pennsylvania ED244711

Bellanca, James. 1990. *The cooperative think tank.* Arlington Heights, IL: SkyLight Training and Publishing, Inc.

Bellanca, James. 1992. *The cooperative think tank II.* Arlington Heights, IL: SkyLight Training and Publishing, Inc.

Bellanca, James and Fogarty, Robin. 1991. *Blueprints for thinking in the cooperative classroom.* Arlington Heights, IL: SkyLight Training and Publishing, Inc.

Benton-Kupper, Jodi. 1999. Can less be more? The quantity versus quality issue of curriculum in a block schedule. *Journal of Research and Development in Education,* 32(3): 168–177.

Berliner, David and Ursula Casanova. 1996. *Putting Research to Work in Your School,* Arlington Heights, IL: IRI/SkyLight Training and Publishing.

Bloom, Benjamin S. and others. 1956. *Taxonomy of Educational Objectives. Handbook 1: Cognitive Domain.* New York: David McKay.

Boyett, Joseph H. with Jimmie T. Boyett. 1995. *Beyond Workplace 2000: Essential Strategies of the Corporation.* New York, NY: Plume Penguine.

Brett, Monroe. 1996. "Teaching Block-Scheduled Class Periods." *The Education Digest,* 62(1), September: 34–37.

Bruer, John T. 1998. Brain science, brain fiction. *Educational Leadership,* 56:3,14–18.

———. 1999. In search of…Brain-based education. *Phi Delta Kappan* 80(9): 649–755.

Burke, Kay. 1992. *Authentic assessment: A collection.* Arlington Heights, IL: SkyLight Training and Publishing, Inc.

———. 1994. *The mindful school: How to assess authentic learning.* Arlington Heights, IL: SkyLight Publishing, Inc.

Buzan, Tony and Barry Buzan. 1994. *The Mind Map Book.* New York: NAL-Dutton.

Cagne, Ellen D., Carol Walker Yekovich, and Frank R. Yekovich. 1993. *The Cognitive Psychology of School Learning.* New York, NY: HarperCollins College Publishers.

Caine, Renate Nummela and Geoffrey Caine. 1991. *Making connections: teaching and the human brain.* Alexandria, VA: Association for Supervision and Curriculum Development.

———. 1997. *Education on the edge of possibility.* Alexandria, VA: Association for Supervision and Curriculum Development.

Caine, Geoffrey, Renate Nummela Caine, and Sam Crowell. 1994. *MindShifts: a brain-based process for restructuring schools and renewing education.* Tucson, AZ: Zephyr Press.

Canady, Robert Lynn. 1990. Parallel block scheduling: A better way to organize a school. *Principal,* 62(3): 34–36.

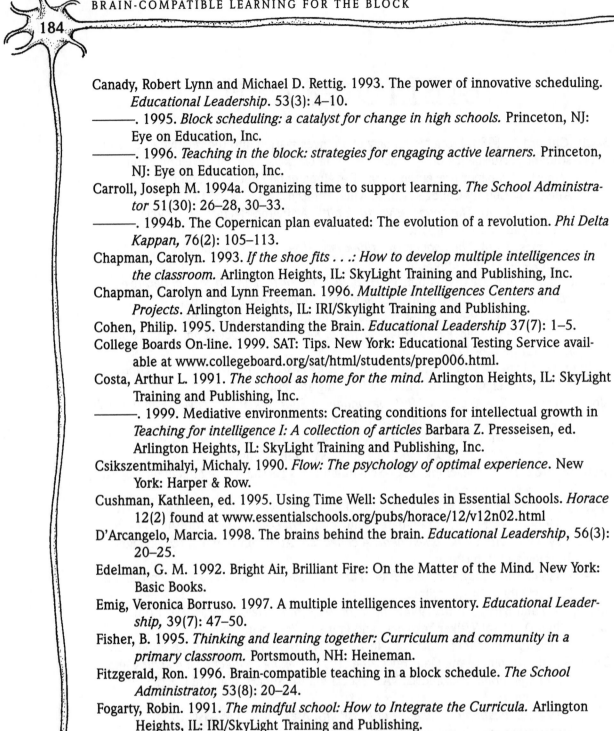

Canady, Robert Lynn and Michael D. Rettig. 1993. The power of innovative scheduling. *Educational Leadership.* 53(3): 4–10.

———. 1995. *Block scheduling: a catalyst for change in high schools.* Princeton, NJ: Eye on Education, Inc.

———. 1996. *Teaching in the block: strategies for engaging active learners.* Princeton, NJ: Eye on Education, Inc.

Carroll, Joseph M. 1994a. Organizing time to support learning. *The School Administrator* 51(30): 26–28, 30–33.

———. 1994b. The Copernican plan evaluated: The evolution of a revolution. *Phi Delta Kappan,* 76(2): 105–113.

Chapman, Carolyn. 1993. *If the shoe fits . . .: How to develop multiple intelligences in the classroom.* Arlington Heights, IL: SkyLight Training and Publishing, Inc.

Chapman, Carolyn and Lynn Freeman. 1996. *Multiple Intelligences Centers and Projects.* Arlington Heights, IL: IRI/Skylight Training and Publishing.

Cohen, Philip. 1995. Understanding the Brain. *Educational Leadership* 37(7): 1–5.

College Boards On-line. 1999. SAT: Tips. New York: Educational Testing Service available at www.collegeboard.org/sat/html/students/prep006.html.

Costa, Arthur L. 1991. *The school as home for the mind.* Arlington Heights, IL: SkyLight Training and Publishing, Inc.

———. 1999. Mediative environments: Creating conditions for intellectual growth in *Teaching for intelligence I: A collection of articles* Barbara Z. Presseisen, ed. Arlington Heights, IL: SkyLight Training and Publishing, Inc.

Csikszentmihalyi, Michaly. 1990. *Flow: The psychology of optimal experience.* New York: Harper & Row.

Cushman, Kathleen, ed. 1995. Using Time Well: Schedules in Essential Schools. *Horace* 12(2) found at www.essentialschools.org/pubs/horace/12/v12n02.html

D'Arcangelo, Marcia. 1998. The brains behind the brain. *Educational Leadership,* 56(3): 20–25.

Edelman, G. M. 1992. Bright Air, Brilliant Fire: On the Matter of the Mind. New York: Basic Books.

Emig, Veronica Borruso. 1997. A multiple intelligences inventory. *Educational Leadership,* 39(7): 47–50.

Fisher, B. 1995. *Thinking and learning together: Curriculum and community in a primary classroom.* Portsmouth, NH: Heineman.

Fitzgerald, Ron. 1996. Brain-compatible teaching in a block schedule. *The School Administrator,* 53(8): 20–24.

Fogarty, Robin. 1991. *The mindful school: How to Integrate the Curricula.* Arlington Heights, IL: IRI/SkyLight Training and Publishing.

———. 1995a. *Best Practices for the Learner-Centered Classroom.* Arlington Heights, IL: SkyLight Training and Publishing.

———. 1995b. *Think about . . . block scheduling.* Arlington Heights, IL: IRI/Skylight Publishing.

———. 1997a. *Brain-compatible classrooms.* Arlington Heights, IL: SkyLight Training and Publishing.

———. 1997b. *Problem-based learning and other curriculum models for the multiple intelligences.* Arlington Heights, IL: Skylight Training and Publishing.

Fogarty, Robin, ed. 1996. *Block scheduling: a collection of articles.* Palatine, IL: IRI/ Skylight Publishing.

Fogarty, Robin and James Bellanca. 1991. *Patterns for thinking patterns for transfer.* Arlington Heights, IL: SkyLight Training and Publishing.

Fogarty, Robin and Judy Stoehr. 1995a. *Integrating curricula with multiple intelligences.* Arlington Heights, IL: SkyLight Training and Publishing.

Gardner, Howard. 1983. *Frames of mind: The theory of multiple intelligences.* New York: Basic Books.

———. 1994. Educating for understanding. *Phi Delta Kappan,* 75(7): 563–565.

———. 1995. Reflections on multiple Intelligences. *Phi Delta Kappan,* 77(10): 200–209.

Given, Barbara K. 1998. Food for thought. *Educational Leadership,* 56(3): 68–71.

Glasser, William. 1986. *Control theory in the classroom.* New York: Perennial Library, Harper & Row, Publishers.

———. 1990. *The quality school.* New York: Perennial Library, Harper & Row, Publishers.

Goleman, Daniel. 1995. *Emotional intelligence.* New York: Bantam Books.

Glenn, H. Stephen and Jane Nelsen. 1988. *Raising self-reliant children in a self-indulgent world.* Rocklin, CA: Prima Publishing & Communications.

Greenwood, C.R., J.C. Dequardi, and R.V. Hall. 1989. Longitudinal effects of classwide peer tutoring. *Journal of Educational Psychology,* 81: 371–383.

Hayes Jacobs, Heidi. 1997. *Mapping the big picture.* Alexandria, VA: Association for Supervision and Curriculum Development.

Hubbard, Barbara Marx. 1998. *Conscious evolution,* Novato, CA: New World Library.

Hugo, Victor. 1992. *Les Miserables,* trans. Charles E. Wilson, reprint, (New York: Modern Library—Random House)

Jensen, Eric. 1998. How Julie's brain learns. *Educational Leadership,* 56(3): 45.

Johnson, David W. and Roger Johnson. 1986. *Circles of learning: Cooperation in the classroom.* Alexandria, VA: Association for Supervision and Curriculum Development.

Johnson, David W., Roger Johnson, and E.J. Holubec. 1988. *Cooperation in the Classroom.* Edina, MN: Interaction Book Company.

Joyce, Bruce, James Wolf, and Emily Calhoun. 1993. *The self-renewing school.* Alexandria, VA: Association of Supervisors and Curriculum Development.

Kendall, James S. and Robert J. Marzano. 1997. *Content knowledge: A compendium of standards and benchmarks for K-12 education* 2d.ed. Alexandria, VA: Association for Supervision and Curriculum Development.

King, Martin Luther, Jr., 1964. *Letter from Birmingham jail.* Philadelphia: American Friends Service Committee.

Kovalik, Susan. 1997. *Integrated thematic instruction: The model,* 3d ed. Kent, WA: Books for Educators, Inc.

Kozulin, Alex and Barbara Z. Presseisen. 1995. Mediated Learning Experience and Psychological Tools: Vygotsky's and Feuerstein's Perspectives in a Study of Student Learning. *Educational Psychologist*, 30: 67–75.

Lazear, David. 1991. *Seven ways of knowing.* Arlington Heights, IL: SkyLight Training and Publishing, Inc.

LeDoux, Joseph. 1996. *The emotional brain: the mysterious underpinnings of emotional life.* New York: Simon & Schuster.

Lee, Harper. 1960. *To kill a mockingbird.* New York: Harper Collins.

Levin, Henry, Gene Glass, and Gail Meister. 1987. Cost effectiveness of computer assisted instruction. *Education Review*, 11 (1987): 50–72.

Lowery, Lawrence. 1998. How new science curriculums reflect brain research. *Educational Leadership*, 56(3): 26–30.

Marshak, David. 1997. *Action research on block scheduling.* Larchmont, NY: Eye on Education.

McTighe, J. and S. Ferrara. 1996. *Assessing learning in the classroom.* Washington D.C.: National Education Association.

National Center for Educational Statistics. 1999. *Educational reform in public elementary and secondary schools: teachers' perspectives.* Washington, D.C.: NCES.

National Education Commission on Time and Learning. 1994. *Prisoners of time.* Washington D.C.: Department of Education, available at www.ed.gov/pubs/PrisonersOfTime/Dimensions.html

O'Day, J., Goertz, M. & Floden, R. 1995. *Building capacity for education reform.* CPRE Policy Briefs, RB-18

Ogle, Donna. 1986. K-W-L group instruction strategy. In A. Palincsar, D. Ogle, B. Jones and E. Carr, eds. *Teaching techniques as thinking (Teleconference resource guide.)* Alexandria, VA: Association for Supervision and Curriculum Development.

Parry, T. and G. Gregory. 1998. *Designing brain compatible learning.* Arlington Heights, IL: SkyLight Training and Publishing Inc.

Pearson, Carol Lynn. 1970. *The search.* Provo, UT: Press Publishing Company.

Rettig, Michael D. and Robert Lynn Canady. 1996. All around the block: the benefits and challenges of a non-traditional school schedule. *The School Administrator,* 53(8): 8–12.

Rosenfield, I. 1988. *The Invention of Memory.* New York: Basic Books.

Roy, P. 1992. Revisiting cooperative learning presentation at outcomes-based education conference November 17, Phoenix, AZ.

Sadowski, Michael. 1996. Just like starting over: The promises and pitfalls of block scheduling. *The Harvard Education Letter,* XII (6): 1–3.

Schmuck, Richard A. 1997. *Practical action research for change.* Arlington Heights, IL: IRI/Skylight Training and Publishing, Inc.

Seifert, E.H. and J. J. Beck. 1984. Relations-ships between task, time, and learning gains in secondary schools. *Journal of Educational Research.* 78 (1984): 5–10.

Semb G.B. and others. 1993. In using time well: schedules in essential schools, ed. Kathleen Cushman. *Horace* 12(2) available at www.essentialschools.org/pubs/horace/12/v12n02.html

Shore, Rebecca. 1995. How one high school improved school climate. *Educational Leadership*, 52(5): 76–78.

Sprenger, Marilee. 1988. Memory lane is a two-way street. *Educational Leadership*, 56(3): 65–67.

Sylwester, Robert. 1995. *A celebration of neurons: an educator's guide to the human brain.* Alexandria, VA: Association for Supervision and Curriculum Development.

Tapscott, D. 1999. Educating the net generation. *Educational Leadership* 56(5): 7–11.

Treadwell, Mark. 1999. *1001 of the best Internet sites for educators.* Arlington Heights, IL: SkyLight Training and Publishing, Inc.

Wassermann, Selma. 1991. Shazam! You're a Teacher. *Phi Delta Kappan*, 80(6): 464–468.

Wheatley, Margaret J. 1992. *Leadership and the new science.* San Francisco, CA: Berrett-Koehler Publishers, Inc.

Wiggins, Grant. 1989. Teaching to the (authentic) test. *Educational Leadership.* 46(7): 41–47.

Williams, R. Bruce. 1993. *More than 50 ways to build team consensus.* Arlington Heights, IL: SkyLight Training and Publishing, Inc.

———. 1997. *Twelve roles of facilitators for school change.* Arlington Heights, IL: SkyLight Training and Publishing, Inc.

Wyatt, Linda D. 1996. More Time, More Training. *The School Administrator,* 53(8): 16–18.

INDEX

There are
one-story intellects,
two-story intellects, and three-story
intellects with skylights. All fact collectors, who
have no aim beyond their facts, are one-story minds. Two-story minds
compare, reason, generalize, using the labors of the fact collectors
as well as their own. Three-story minds idealize, imagine,
predict—their best illumination comes from
above, through the skylight.
—*Oliver Wendell*
Holmes